# the
# golden pear
# cafe
# cookbook

# the golden pear cafe cookbook

### easy, luscious recipes for brunch and more from the Hamptons' favorite cafe

## Keith E. Davis

THOMAS DUNNE BOOKS
St. Martin's Press ❧ New York

THOMAS DUNNE BOOKS.
An imprint of St. Martin's Press.

THE GOLDEN PEAR CAFE COOKBOOK. Copyright © 2006 by Keith E. Davis. Foreword copyright © by Dan Rattiner. All rights reserved. Printed in the United States of America. No part of this book may be used or reproduced in any manner whatsoever without written permission except in the case of brief quotations embodied in critical articles or reviews. For information, address St. Martin's Press, 175 Fifth Avenue, New York, N.Y. 10010.

www.stmartins.com

Photographs by Jim Lennon. Copyright © Brenner-Lennon 2005.
Design by Kathryn Parise

LIBRARY OF CONGRESS CATALOGING-IN-PUBLICATION DATA

Davis, Keith E.
    The Golden Pear Cafe cookbook : easy, luscious recipes for brunch and more from the Hamptons' favorite cafe / Keith E. Davis.
        p.  cm.
    ISBN 0-312-34971-8
    EAN 978-0-312-34971-4
    1. Brunches.  2. Golden Pear Cafe.  I. Golden Pear Cafe.  II. Title.

TX733.D38 2006
641.5'32—dc22

                                                          2006040163

First Edition: May 2006

10  9  8  7  6  5  4  3  2  1

*To my parents, James Arnold and Barbara Davis,*
*with the greatest love, respect, and thanks*

# contents

## 6 · bakery treats   123

## 7 · basics   153

## 8 · appendix   169

# acknowledgments

The projects in our lives that require a concerted effort between people depend heavily upon strong relationships. This book is the result of a number of such relationships, some long-term, some short; some a collaboration of sorts between the divine and human. This book is an outstanding example of how working together in harmony can produce something really special.

Therefore, I first want to thank God for this book. Without Him there wouldn't be the Golden Pear Cafe. He has guided and directed my life from the day I was born, and just about everything we sell is from His good creation, whether food or drink.

My wife, Anne, has been my best fan and food critic for the past seventeen years. She has a keen sense of quality when it comes to food, and that has been a great asset to me. She has tirelessly supported me and provided objective feedback on the quality of our menu items, even while raising our three children. She has assisted me with this business from day one, and it is only fitting that we are called the Golden Pear (read pair). She is my soul mate and partner, forever! I love you.

My children, Sarah, Emily, and Keith, are such a joy. They love each other and are excellent students who make their mother and me so very proud. I love the fact that they enjoy baking at home and eating good food (most of the time). I love you guys—and like I always say, "Go easy on the cookies."

Although my parents, James Arnold and Barbara Davis, were not foodies or gourmands, they were hard workers who loved me and taught me a great deal during my formative years. They supported me when I left the engineering field for a career in food service, and my mom worked many hours at the Golden Pear in Southampton during our first fourteen years in business. They instilled in me the idea that a strong marriage is more important than anything else. I love you and I thank you.

My sincere thanks go to my brother, Tim, and Susan, his wife, for opening their beautiful home for much of the photography in this book.

Many thanks to all the members of the Golden Pear Cafe team, who work endlessly to serve our beloved customers.

Karen Berman, the editor of this book, has done a fabulous job. It has been such a pleasure working with you on this book. The editorial process was new and challenging to me, and writing, editing, and reading the recipes in these pages has given me a new understanding of cookbooks. Thanks for smoothing everything out and making it sound so perfect. You're the best!

I am so glad to have met and hired Robert Tebinka to be executive chef of the Golden Pear. He has helped elevate our operations and menus so that we continue to be the very best in the Hamptons. His unwavering help in adapting many of our recipes for the home cook has made this book possible—and he made it fun, which is so important. We laughed and joked often, and that made this project a positive experience for both of us. Thank you!

Special thanks to my talented assistant, Gina Biamonte, who helped in the preparation of the manuscript while keeping our office running smoothly.

Jim Lennon, his wife, Mona, and their friend and food stylist Leslie Baxter did an amazing job with the photography for this book. Jim's talent, style, and lighting expertise gave such beauty to our food and its surroundings.

My thanks go out to Noah Lukeman for believing in me and the Golden Pear Cafe and for moving this project into reality. Without him this book would not exist.

When I learned that John *Parsley* would be our editor at St. Martin's Press, I knew we got the right guy. *Well, with a name like that,* I thought, *what a great omen.* Just as parsley is a very useful, colorful, important ingredient in cooking, so was John with this book. He guided and shaped our thoughts as we began to pull things together, and the result is fantastic.

Peter Collins has been my business adviser for a few years now, and he guided and encouraged me to write this book, especially during the initial phase. Thank you for your help, Peter.

A few years ago, I was considering changing my primary food supplier. It was then I met John King, owner of J. King's Foodservice. He's a guy who's just as passionate, if not more, about food and business. I am so glad that we work together. He's been a great asset and close friend, and he helped me make this book possible. Thanks, John.

Finally, to all the Golden Pear Cafe fans, I send you the warmest, most heartfelt *thank you*. For eighteen years you have supported my business and provided me with countless memories, feedback, and joy. My life is so full, knowing and serving you all. I look forward to serving you for many more years at the Golden Pear Cafes.

# foreword

by Dan Rattiner, *Dan's Papers*

One of the many things that drew me to the beautiful old New England–style beach towns they call the Hamptons forty-five years ago were the luncheonettes and diners where people congregated. In those early days, before the Hamptons got entirely citified with celebrities and Wall Street types, the local people would read the newspapers and hold court in places such as the Candy Kitchen in Bridgehampton, the Sip 'n Soda in Southampton, and Eddie's Luncheonette in East Hampton. Two of these three soldier on today, but eighteen years ago, as the Hamptons expanded and the population grew to be a virtual sixth borough of New York City, Keith Davis got the idea that the community needed a new kind of meeting place to supplement the old—and so he founded the first of his Golden Pears, a more urban coffee-cafe meeting place now in a chain that includes locations in East Hampton, Bridgehampton, Southampton, and Stony Brook.

I've never been quite sure where the name came from, and I have never asked, and the reason is that the name has come to signify the place itself. Golden Pears are Golden Pears.

The Golden Pear provides the very best of the city and the best of the country. It is primarily visited for breakfast or lunch, but coffee will do, and they have interesting early dinners. There are the morning papers for sale, and there are cafe tables and chairs—so it is part do-it-yourself coffee and cappucino bar, part deli, part bakery, and part meet your friends. Deals are done at the Golden Pear, friends are made, stories are told, advice is offered, and people who have had their feathers ruffled can get them unruffled at the Golden Pear.

I kind of caught myself up when I said deli, because you can spend a morning in town thinking about the citrus veggie tuna salad wrap you are going to have for lunch at the Golden Pear or the grilled wild salmon salad with asparagus and dijon dill. This is some deli. You can eat there, you can take out to the beach, or you can take it home. What do they put in that butternut squash and apple soup? You will find the answers in this book.

You will also learn the recipes to some of their many imaginative breakfasts such as farmhouse frittata, or to their fresh baked goods that include cranberry walnut muffins, raisin spice muffins, and chocolate–chocolate chip loaf cake.

The Golden Pears have thrived, and it is difficult now to imagine the community without them. Along with, I suppose, *Dan's Papers*, they are the heart of the Hamptons.

# introduction

The night before I opened the Golden Pear Cafe in 1987, it snowed. People had said I was crazy for opening a cafe in a summer resort community like the Hamptons in November, but the location was available, and after years of working in other people's food businesses, I was determined to have a place of my own. I had decided that we should open on a Thursday to get a day of practice before the weekend, and I set the date for November 12. I can't remember snow falling that early in the season in any year before or since, but on the night of November 11, hours before our first morning of business, six inches of snow poured out of the sky. A few members of my staff and I were still stocking shelves, pricing products, and cooking when it started to snow. We worked for a while longer, and then I sent everyone home. I fell asleep on a couch in the basement and spent a restless night dreaming about my opening day and all the steps that had led me to this moment.

I remembered my first day of school in the eleventh grade. At the end of English class, my teacher, Mrs. Gaspari, had announced that a local restaurant was looking for a dishwasher. I needed a job, so when the bell rang, I went straight to her desk. She handed me a piece of paper, and after school I read the address and headed over to the Albatross Seafood restaurant in Shirley, New York. I was hired on the spot, and over the next two years I not only washed dishes but shucked clams (I could open a dozen clams faster than anybody I ever knew or heard of), cleaned mussels, worked the deep fryer, and helped out wherever help was needed. My hands were always raw. I was quarterback of my high school football team, and it hurt to grip the football with fingers split open from detergent and clamshells. Still, there was something about working in a restaurant that was irresistible—the pace, the energy, the satisfaction of seeing people enjoy food that I had helped prepare.

Back then, I couldn't have known that an after-school dishwashing job would lead me to a career in restaurants that would span more than twenty-five years—but here we are. As proprietor of the Golden Pear Cafes, I have the pleasure of serving food that is (I like to think) delicious and innovative. Three of our cafes are located in one of the most glamorous resort destinations in America—the Hamptons—and I thoroughly enjoy my fly-on-the-wall vantage point, observing all the fun. Now, with this book, I have the opportunity to share some of our best-loved recipes, along with a few stories of life in the Hamptons. I decided to make brunch the organizing principle of this book because our menu at the Golden Pear allows customers to order breakfast and lunch all day long. Fluffy omelets, spicy breakfast burritos, hearty oatmeal, sandwiches and panini, soups, salads, and hot and cold main dishes are all available any time of day. We are the quintessential brunch stop in the Hamptons, and nothing typifies the Hamptons lifestyle like brunch.

Brunch is relaxed, easy, infinitely adaptable—and as casual or as elegant as you want it to be. Dine lightly or make a feast of it. Choose breakfast or lunch or a bit of both. Linger as long as you like: At brunch, time stands still and Monday morning is eons away. It's all about enjoying food with family and friends—or, if you prefer, just the Sunday papers. In short, brunch can be anything—as long as there's food involved. I guess that's why I like it.

I suppose you could apply that phrase "anything—as long as there's food involved" to my entire career. I was so taken with all that I learned as a dishwasher at the Albatross that I continued to work in restaurants and catering companies throughout high school and college. I earned a degree in electrical engineering, but even as I went through my courses, I knew my heart would never be in that field. As luck would have it, a chef friend called me after graduation about a job in a gourmet store. That job led to another, and on a summer day in 1987 I learned from a coworker about a restaurant that was going to be sold. I knew of that restaurant—it had a prime location on the busiest corner of downtown Southampton. That was in July. I took over the property on October 1, and by November, christened with six inches of snow, the Golden Pear was open for business.

I like to think of the way the cafe's name, the Golden Pear, came about as a sign. When I began to prepare for my own opening, I initially hired a friend to work the counter while I cooked and baked in the back. Together, we'd be a pair—a golden pair—which morphed into Golden Pear. I liked the sound of it. I even had business cards made. Even so, I wasn't totally sure it was the right name until the day, shortly before my scheduled opening, when my mom came home from church and said, "You *have* to call it the Golden Pear." In her hand was a church bulletin that bore the quotation: "All things work together for good with those that love God"—Romans 8:28. Above it was a picture of a hand with a pear in it. The cafe was officially named.

With a location and a name, I began to develop the concept. I decided on a combination restaurant and specialty food store selling fresh baked goods, great coffee, salads, sandwiches, soups, and entrees for take-out and eat-in. I wanted to take classic American dishes and give them a healthy gourmet twist. Our blueberry muffins would have less sugar, and we would use a bit of whole-wheat flour in them. Our chicken salad would not have mayonnaise but a less fattening honey mustard dressing. Our sandwiches would be made with the freshest breads available and the highest quality meats and cheeses. Our breakfast specials would be served with fresh fruit, our omelets would be filled with fresh vegetables, and our oatmeal would be old-fashioned and topped with fresh berries.

I had borrowed every penny that I could to prepare for the opening. I fixed up the place myself, with the help of a few friends. I met with a legion of vendors and purveyors to find the very best for each ingredient. I was working twelve to fifteen hours a day, but I wanted everything to be just right. As the big day approached, things began to come together. Then came Black

Monday, the stock market crash of October 1987. I was concerned, to say the least, as many regular Hamptons vacationers had suffered significant losses. We were relieved when the markets recovered a few days later, but it took two years for recovery to reach previous bull-market levels, and the crash hardly made for an auspicious opening date. And there were more challenges to come.

When I awoke at 5:00 A.M. on my cafe's opening morning, the ground was covered. What could I do? I began baking croissants, muffins, and cookies and brewing coffee. By 8:00 A.M., I was busy preparing salads. Miraculously, when it was just about time to open the doors, I looked outside—and the snow was beginning to melt. My fear that my first day in business would be a total disaster melted away with the snow, especially when our first customers began to come in. It was an exciting day, an exhausting day full of uncertainties, but when we closed shop at five o'clock that evening we could declare it a success.

From that day on, our reputation began to spread around the village. We were busier and busier each day. People really liked our food and our style of friendly, efficient service. I had a small crew of four, and they did a wonderful job. Customers would tell me what they liked and disliked and what foods they thought we should add to the menu. I took as much of their advice as I could and went to work on creating some new menu items. One thing they wanted, since it was winter, was hot food. I added a steam table setup and soon began to serve soups and other hot lunches. One soup that I created back then was our Country Chicken Soup, chock full of vegetables and touched with fragrant rosemary. It sold well all winter and into the spring. In fact, we still sell gallons of the stuff.

We made it through that winter, and when spring came and business was picking up, I realized I had to hire a full-time baker. I chose a New York Restaurant School graduate named Anne Adams. Soon, our business name's root—the golden pair—took on a new meaning for me. Anne and I worked together developing new bakery products, and by July we were dating. We got engaged in December and married in February—in the off-season, of course. We worked side by side until 1990, when we became the parents of Sarah. Two more children followed: Emily in 1993 and Keith in 1995. Anne still helps out in the office a few days a week, and she still loves to bake at home, revealing little baking secrets to our children. Many of her recipes—the Chocolumps™, her wonderful brownies and blondies, and her Lemon Loaf Cake—are still top sellers.

In the meantime, the Golden Pear Cafe has continued to grow. On New Year's Day 1991, the cafe was closed for the day, and Anne and I indulged in a rare treat: an afternoon drive. In East Hampton, we noticed a FOR LEASE sign in the window of an old cafe. Purely by coincidence, a few days later, the cafe owner's son came to see me and asked if I was interested in the space. I was, so I went to see it, and I liked what I saw—and my decision was made when I walked down into the basement and saw a huge Botero print of a golden pear. Another sign! The second Golden Pear opened on the site later that year.

More branches followed: one in Bridgehampton in 1996 and another in the Village of Old Stony Brook on the North Shore of Long Island in 1998.

Our original menu has expanded exponentially, and we now have a corporate chef to oversee operations for all four kitchens, but the recipe for our success hasn't changed. We still work hard to make and serve the best food we can. From May through September, the crowds start piling in at around 10:00 A.M. for late breakfasts and take-out lunches for a beautiful day at the beach. On days when inclement weather keeps them away from the water, hungry patrons crowd the village streets and pile into the Golden Pear for lunch. The staff works at top speed to get the food out to lines of customers that seem endless while prepping catering orders at the same time. Once September comes, the pace slows, but business is still steady, and that's when we test recipes and gear up for the madness that spring will bring.

Life chugs along, and through it all the Golden Pear remains as I envisioned it—an intimate, friendly neighborhood cafe serving only the best, freshest, most delicious food and drink possible. Now, I'm pleased to have the opportunity to share it all with you in this book. Here in the Hamptons, great brunches—whether big and glamorous or cozy and intimate—are a way of life. You might not have an ocean beach in your backyard or a celebrity living in the house next door, but with the recipes in this book, you can have a Hamptons-style brunch any time you like, the Golden Pear way.

# 1 · coffee

## Hot Property

I like to say that the four-foot by four-foot areas occupied by our coffee bars are among the most valuable pieces of real estate in the Hamptons. People love our coffee—and they'll endure long lines to get some. On summer mornings at our Southampton shop, people queue up inside, out the door, and around the corner waiting for their steaming Golden Pear cups. I think—if I do say so myself—that their devotion is entirely justified; we've worked long and hard to learn what makes a good cup of java, and ours is the freshest in the village.

All kinds of little dramas play out at the Golden Pear coffee stations. If you hang around long enough, you're sure to witness something that will leave you chuckling for the rest of the day. For example, Carol Friedland, a good

◄ The Golden Pear Cafe—Bridgehampton

7

friend and longtime customer of the Golden Pear in East Hampton, is a clinical psychologist who has appeared on lots of TV talk shows: Ricki Lake, Montel Williams, Maury Povich, and the like. One morning she was pouring herself a cup of coffee when Alec Baldwin appeared next to her.

At that moment, one of my newer, younger employees recognized Carol and blurted out, "You're Dr. Carol! I saw you on the Ricki Lake show yesterday! Can I have your autograph?" Carol looked at the handsome actor standing next to her, then back at the staffer and said, "Hey, if you really want someone's autograph, you should get his."

The staffer stared into Alec Baldwin's eyes—and shook her head. "Who are you?" she asked. "I don't know you." Carol proceeded to introduce Alec Baldwin, famous movie star and Broadway actor.

"Never heard of him," the staffer replied.

Carol started to apologize, but Alec, ever the gentleman, broke into a grin. "Nothing to be sorry about," he said. He thought the whole thing was pretty funny and proceeded to get his coffee. The moral of the story: Celebrity might be in the eye of the beholder, but good coffee puts a smile on every face.

# The Perfect Cup

Everybody has a different idea of the perfect cup of coffee, and coffee styles differ from place to place. Some like their coffee as thin as tea, while others enjoy it as thick as mud. My produce supplier was Turkish. One day he invited my wife and me over for a cup of coffee. What a surprise—his coffee was dark and thick. I tried to make it more palatable with some milk and sugar, but it wasn't my idea of coffee. Of course, I tried to drink the whole thing—I didn't want to offend him—and I learned that coffee is, well, on the tongue of the beholder.

Coffee is a matter of personal taste, but over the years I've picked up a few tidbits that hold true whether you like your coffee strong or weak, with cream or fat-free milk, with sugar or black.

**Beans:** At the Golden Pear we use 100 percent Arabica beans from Colombia. We like the Colombian Supremo, the largest variety, and we get them roasted to perfection, with the classic American roasting technique. Over the years, they've been our customers' favorite, and I really think they are the best. That's because they're grown at such high altitudes, so they take longer to mature and consequently have more time to develop and concentrate their flavor. I suggest that you look for Colombian Supremo, but you should also try other beans and blends to find your favorite. Whichever bean or blend you buy, ask when it was roasted. It's worthwhile to shop around for a reputable coffee shop or cafe to find the freshest coffee; it makes a difference in the flavor and aroma. Also, avoid buying loose coffee beans that are stored in wall units or open barrels. Coffee beans lose much of their aroma within a few days of being exposed to the open air. Beans sold in sealed bags, while less picturesque, retain their aroma better. Then, when you get your coffee home, store it properly, in an airtight container that you keep in a cool, dry spot. Don't store your beans in the refrigerator, because the coffee will absorb flavors and aromas from other foods. You can freeze coffee, but only if you're not going to use it within a two-week period. If you buy coffee that is sold in sealed bags with a valve that allows gases to escape, you can store it unopened for up to three months. Once you open it, however, you should transfer the beans to an airtight container.

**Grinding:** I recommend buying whole beans and grinding them yourself, or having them ground in the store. If you choose the latter option, you'll find that most commercial coffee grinders have designated settings for different grinds, so your beans will be ground to just the right texture and consistency. If you grind your beans at home—and I urge you to try it; there's really nothing like grinding your coffee immediately before you brew it because the volatile oils expressed in the grinding lose potency when exposed for any length of time—your grinder probably won't be so precise, so test the grind a few times to get it just right. When you grind your coffee beans for an automatic drip machine, the result should feel like granulated sugar. If you are using a French press, the coffee should be ground more coarsely. Espresso beans should be ground to a very fine powder.

**Brewing:** I believe filtered water makes a huge difference; particularly if you use tap water, all the junk that's in it can interfere with the flavor of the cup. Likewise, brewing temperature is key: Make sure your machine brews coffee at the perfect temperature, which is 195 degrees F. Finally, be sure to use filters that fit your brew basket; if you don't, in addition to having inferior coffee, you'll have a mess to clean up. Try to purchase unbleached filters or gold-plated wire-mesh ones. Both are environmentally friendly.

You can adjust these measurements to your liking, but I recommend the following proportions of coffee to water:

| Coffee | Water |
|---|---|
| 1½ to 2 tablespoons | 6 ounces (¾ cup) |
| 2 to 2½ tablespoons | 8 ounces (1 cup) |
| Espresso | Water |
| 2 heaping tablespoons | 4 ounces (½ cup) |

Finally, at the Golden Pear any coffee that hasn't sold in thirty minutes— it happens occasionally—is thrown out; old coffee loses flavor. We wouldn't dream of doing otherwise.

# espresso

*makes 1 (4-ounce) cup*

"Espresso" is one of the most misunderstood terms in the coffee business. Some think it means beans that have been roasted until they are very dark, while others think it's a kind of bean imported from Italy. Both are incorrect. "Espresso" is a method of brewing in which hot water is quickly infused with finely ground coffee, either on a stovetop or in an espresso machine. Espresso can be made with light or dark-roasted beans of any variety. Try this recipe at home, and if it's not perfect the first time, give it another try. It will take some practice. Remember that the perfect espresso should have the famous crema *after brewing—the creamy beige substance floating on the top.* Crema *has nothing to do with dairy-based cream. It's what happens naturally to the espresso when it's brewed.*

2 heaping tablespoons finely
   ground espresso

½ cup water, preferably filtered

Sugar or other sweetener to taste,
   optional

Fresh lemon rind, cut into a 1-inch-
   by-¼-inch sliver, optional

Gently pack the ground coffee into your espresso maker's brewing basket. Secure the basket in the machine's brewing head. Add the water according to the espresso machine manufacturer's instructions. Brew the espresso and let it flow into a small espresso cup or, if you are going to make cappuccino (see page 12), into a shot glass.

If you wish, add sugar or sweetener to taste or float a piece of fresh lemon rind in the espresso for 15 to 20 seconds.

# cappuccino

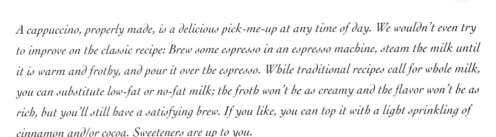

*makes 2 (16-ounce) mugs*

*A cappuccino, properly made, is a delicious pick-me-up at any time of day. We wouldn't even try to improve on the classic recipe: Brew some espresso in an espresso machine, steam the milk until it is warm and frothy, and pour it over the espresso. While traditional recipes call for whole milk, you can substitute low-fat or no-fat milk; the froth won't be as creamy and the flavor won't be as rich, but you'll still have a satisfying brew. If you like, you can top it with a light sprinkling of cinnamon and/or cocoa. Sweeteners are up to you.*

4 heaping tablespoons finely
   ground espresso
1 cup water, preferably filtered
1½ cups whole milk
Sugar or other sweetener to taste,
   optional

Ground cinnamon to taste, optional
Unsweetened cocoa powder to
   taste, optional

Brew the espresso according to the manufacturer's instructions and divide it between 2 large coffee mugs.

Pour the milk into a stainless steel frothing pitcher. Steam and froth the milk until it is very warm (160 degrees F.).

Slowly pour equal portions of steamed milk into the mugs, holding back the frothy foam with a tablespoon. If you are using sweetener, add it and stir to dissolve it. Then scoop the froth out of the frothing pitcher and ladle it over the top of each mug; if you're feeling artistic, make a few frothy peaks.

If you wish, sprinkle the top of each cappuccino with cinnamon and/or cocoa powder to taste.

# cafe latte

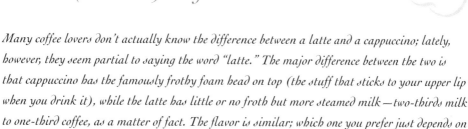

*makes 2 (16-ounce) mugs*

*Many coffee lovers don't actually know the difference between a latte and a cappuccino; lately, however, they seem partial to saying the word "latte." The major difference between the two is that cappuccino has the famously frothy foam head on top (the stuff that sticks to your upper lip when you drink it), while the latte has little or no froth but more steamed milk—two-thirds milk to one-third coffee, as a matter of fact. The flavor is similar; which one you prefer just depends on whether you like the froth.*

4 heaping tablespoons ground
  espresso
1 cup water, preferably filtered
2 cups whole milk
Sugar or other sweetener to taste,
  optional

Ground cinnamon to taste, optional
Unsweetened cocoa powder to
  taste, optional

> *TIP: To avoid making froth when you steam the milk, immerse the steam wand to the bottom of the frothing pitcher and keep it there.*

Brew the espresso according to the manufacturer's instructions and divide it between 2 large coffee mugs.

Pour the milk into a stainless steel frothing pitcher, positioning the steaming wand at the bottom of the pitcher to prevent froth from forming. Steam the milk until it is very warm (160 degrees F.).

Slowly pour equal portions of the steamed milk into the mugs. If you are using sweetener, add it and stir to dissolve it.

If you wish, sprinkle the top of each cafe latte with cinnamon and/or cocoa to taste.

# cafe mocha

*makes 2 (16-ounce) mugs*

*A cafe mocha is essentially a chocolate cappuccino, and it happens to be my personal favorite. The recipe is pretty much the same as for cappuccino, except that you add chocolate syrup to the milk and froth them together to create a delicious, chocolaty beverage. The syrup is sweet enough that you won't need any additional sweeteners. Good old Hershey's chocolate syrup works really well in cafe mocha; we've been using it at the Golden Pear Cafe for years.*

4 heaping tablespoons ground
   espresso
1 cup water, preferably filtered
4 tablespoons chocolate syrup

1½ cups whole milk
Whipped cream to taste, optional
Unsweetened cocoa powder to
   taste, optional

> *TIP: You can add fruit syrups and other flavorings to your coffee if you wish. Like the chocolate used in cafe mocha, these syrups are pretty sweet, so I recommend that you start by adding just one tablespoon per eight-ounce cup of coffee or cappuccino. Taste it, and if you have a real sweet tooth, you can add more.*

Brew the espresso according to the manufacturer's instructions and divide it between 2 large coffee mugs.

Pour the chocolate syrup into the stainless steel frothing pitcher. Add the milk. Steam and froth the milk until it is very warm (160 degrees F.).

Slowly pour equal portions of the steamed chocolate milk into the mugs, holding back the frothy foam with a tablespoon. Then scoop the froth out of the frothing pitcher and ladle it over the top of each mug; if you're feeling artistic, make a few frothy peaks.

If you wish, spoon some whipped cream on top and sprinkle each of the cafe mochas with cocoa powder to taste.

# 2 · breakfast

## A Summer Sunday in Southampton

There is nothing quite like a Sunday morning in July at the Golden Pear in Southampton. The staff arrives at 6:00 A.M. to get the cafe ready for the tidal wave of caffeine-seeking Hamptonites who will soon arrive. Most of our staff are still tired from the gangbuster business we did on Saturday. A few extra shots of espresso perk

◄ Garden Vegetable Egg-White Omelet

them up, and the adrenaline builds as 7:00 A.M.—opening time—approaches.

Copies of the Sunday *New York Times* and the glossy *Hamptons Magazine* are stacked up in towering piles. The bakery display is packed full with freshly baked croissants, cinnamon buns, muffins, and crumb cakes. (The baking crew was up most of the night preparing all the goodies.) The kitchen team is like a bunch of runners awaiting the start of a marathon. Eggs are cracked, whisked, and ready to go for omelets, breakfast burritos, and our famous Scrambled Eggs and Cheddar Cheese on Croissants. Waffle machines ready . . . go!

The coffee and cappuccino machines are squealing. The cappuccino/latte bar is stocked with whole milk, 2 percent milk, skim milk, and soy milk, as well as sugar, various sweeteners, cinnamon, and cocoa. (Sometimes I wonder about the demand for so many different kinds of milk and sweetener, but we'll do anything to please our customers!) Half of the crowd that will arrive for the morning ritual has been out most of the night socializing, whisking from one party to the next, with stops at trendy local nightspots. They usually need an extra shot of espresso in their latte. The rest—families with kids, and others who keep to their early-to-bed habits even in the Hamptons—will do just fine with a regular dose of caffeine.

We unlock the doors at seven o'clock sharp, and the crowd piles in. There's a flurry of activity as customers try to grab the tables overlooking Main Street. The counter crew takes breakfast orders as quickly as possible and punches them into our computer system, which transmits them to the kitchen. There, the chefs begin to cook at an amazingly fast pace. Out front, the bagel toaster is jammed full; it will remain that way for the next five hours. Customers mob the service counter with special requests.

"Can I get two oatmeal specials and two breakfast burritos to go, and hurry up because I've got to get to the beach and get a parking space."

"Six everything bagels scooped out and toasted well done with light cream cheese."

"I'll have the Belgian waffle, but can you put everything on the side?"

By 9:30 the place is full to capacity, and customers have formed a line out the door. The staffers are doing everything that they can to meet what feels like an insatiable, unending demand. It's mayhem—but controlled mayhem.

In other words, a typical Sunday morning in July at the Golden Pear.

# farmhouse frittata

. . . . . . . . . . . . . . . . . . . . . . . . . . . . .

*makes 10 to 12 servings*

*This is the perfect egg dish for your brunch buffet. The combination of ingredients is savory and satisfying and makes for a delicate, melt-in-your-mouth texture. Be sure to use high-quality breakfast sausage and find a good farmhouse Cheddar at your local cheese shop or gourmet store—or order some online. Bake the frittata in a pretty casserole dish and it can go right from the oven to the buffet.*

¾ stick (6 tablespoons) unsalted butter

16 large eggs

¾ cup heavy cream

2 tablespoons plus 1 teaspoon fresh chopped parsley

1 tablespoon fresh thyme leaves

2 teaspoons kosher salt

¼ teaspoon freshly ground black pepper

6 large or 12 small breakfast sausages (about 10 ounces)

1½ cups diced onion (about ¾ medium onion)

3 cups baby bella mushrooms, trimmed

6 ripe medium plum tomatoes, cored, seeded, and cut into ¼-inch chunks (about 3 cups)

1½ cups grated extra-sharp farmhouse Cheddar cheese (6 ounces)

Fresh parsley sprigs, for garnish

Fresh strawberries, for garnish

Orange slices, for garnish

> **TIP:** *Sauté is a French word that literally means "to leap." In cooking, when you sauté, you cook something—usually vegetables, meat, or poultry—in a shallow pan with just a few spoons of fat, stirring it and shaking the pan so that the food does not stick to the bottom (in whimsical terms, it leaps). If you cook until the food is tender but not colored, that's called "sweating" it. If you cook until it caramelizes (releases its natural sugars) and becomes golden to golden brown, that's sautéing.*

Preheat the oven to 450 degrees F. Grease a 9 × 14 × 3-inch casserole dish with 2 tablespoons of butter.

. . . . . . . . . . . . . . . . . . . . . . . . . . . . . . . . . . . .

Crack the eggs into a large mixing bowl. Add the cream, 2 tablespoons of chopped parsley, and the thyme, salt, and pepper and whisk the ingredients vigorously for 1 minute or until they are thoroughly combined. Set it aside.

Place the breakfast sausages on a sheet pan and roast them for 15 minutes. Remove them from the pan and set them aside to cool. When the sausages are cool enough to handle, transfer them to a work surface and chop them coarsely. Set them aside.

Meanwhile, melt the remaining 4 tablespoons of butter in a large saucepan set over medium heat and swirl the pan to coat the surface. Add the onions and sauté them, stirring them and shaking the pan, for 3 minutes or until they are soft and translucent. Add the mushrooms and sauté the mixture, stirring it frequently, for 1 minute. Add the tomatoes and sauté it, stirring, for 3 minutes longer.

Spoon the sausage and the vegetable mixture into the prepared casserole and spread this mixture evenly with a wooden spoon so that it covers the bottom of the dish. Sprinkle the Cheddar cheese evenly over the top. Pour in the egg mixture. Using a wooden spoon or spatula, fold the frittata mixture to combine the ingredients completely and spread it evenly in the casserole.

Place the casserole in the center of the oven and bake it for 15 minutes; then rotate the casserole 180 degrees to ensure even baking. Bake it for 15 minutes longer or until an instant-read thermometer inserted into the center of the frittata reads 165 degrees F. Remove the casserole from the oven and sprinkle it with the remaining 1 teaspoon of chopped parsley.

To serve, place the casserole on a warming tray on your buffet table or cut the frittata into 3-inch squares and serve them on individual plates. Garnish each serving with fresh parsley sprigs, a strawberry, and an orange slice.

*Time for Brunch: You can prepare the frittata 1 hour in advance and hold it in a 170-degree oven. Refrigerate any leftovers for up to 3 days; microwave them for a few minutes to reheat them.*

# garden vegetable
# egg-white omelet

*makes 2 omelets*

*One summer morning I was working in our Bridgehampton cafe when Calvin Klein came in with a friend. He stepped up to the counter and ordered this omelet, plus a croissant and our Organic Yogurt with Banana, Berries, and Maple Granola. I thought that was breakfast for the two of them, but then his friend ordered her own omelet. I kidded Calvin that he should probably head to the gym after breakfast. He replied politely that he had already walked several miles on the beach. "I'm famished," he said. I guess if anybody knows how to fit into a pair of Calvins, he does—and really, you can't do too much damage to your diet with this light but satisfying omelet. If you wish, use nonstick canola oil spray instead of butter to make it even lighter. You can also substitute diced asparagus or diced green peppers for the broccoli.*

12 small broccoli florets

1 tablespoon plus 1 teaspoon
   unsalted butter

½ small zucchini, diced (about
   ½ cup)

½ small yellow squash, diced (about
   ½ cup)

2 ripe medium plum tomatoes,
   seeded and diced (about 1 cup)

1 scallion, chopped

1 tablespoon plus 1 teaspoon
   chopped fresh parsley

Kosher salt to taste

Freshly ground black pepper to
   taste

8 large egg whites, lightly beaten

*TIP: Blanching vegetables softens them just enough so that they are easier to chew and digest and sets their color to a brilliant hue. The process is easy: Immerse the broccoli (or whatever you are blanching) in boiling water for about thirty seconds and then in ice water for another thirty seconds. The key to blanching is speed; remove the vegetable immediately from both the hot and cold water.*

Preheat the broiler to high and position a rack about 6 inches from the broiling element.

Blanch the broccoli: Boil a saucepan of water and prepare a bowl of ice water. Immerse the broccoli in the boiling water for 20 to 30 seconds. Using a slotted spoon, transfer it to the ice water and immerse it for 30 seconds. Drain it and set it aside.

Melt 2 teaspoons of butter in an 8-inch nonstick ovenproof sauté pan set over medium-high heat and swirl the pan to coat the surface. Add the broccoli florets, zucchini, yellow squash, tomatoes, and scallions and sauté them, stirring them and shaking the pan, for 2 to 3 minutes or until they are just tender. Add the parsley, salt, and pepper and stir the mixture to blend it. With a slotted spoon, transfer the vegetables to a small bowl. Set them aside. Wipe the pan clean with a paper towel.

Heat the remaining 2 teaspoons of butter until it is melted and the pan is hot. Pour in half of the egg whites and tilt the pan to coat the bottom. Using a spatula, gently lift the edges of the omelet so that the uncooked, still-liquid egg whites flow to the bottom of the pan and the omelet takes the pan's circular shape. Cook the omelet for 1 minute. Transfer the pan to the oven and broil the omelet for 20 to 30 seconds or until the eggs are cooked through. Carefully remove the pan from the broiler and spoon half of the vegetables over the omelet. Return the pan to the broiler and broil the omelet for 30 seconds longer. Remove the pan from the oven and gently slide the omelet out of it, folding it in half onto the plate as you do so. Keep it warm and repeat the process with the remaining ingredients to make another omelet.

*Time for Brunch: You can prep the vegetables ahead of time, but the omelet itself is best made just before you plan to serve it.*

# the ultimate breakfast burrito

*makes 4 whole burritos, 8 half burritos, or
16 quarter burritos*

*I introduced this breakfast special a few summers ago, and it quickly became a top seller. The combination of chorizo sausage, Cheddar cheese, and salsa makes a welcome addition to an intimate brunch or a larger buffet. The recipe multiplies easily to suit the size of your guest list. Our own salsa, coupled with the chorizo, gives the dish a pleasantly hot one-two punch.*

1 tablespoon plus 1 teaspoon
   unsalted butter
2 large (4-ounce) links precooked
   chorizo sausage
8 large eggs, lightly beaten
1 cup grated farmhouse Cheddar
   cheese (4 ounces)
½ cup Spicy Tomato Salsa (see page
   160), or mild tomato salsa from

the supermarket's refrigerated section
2 scallions, chopped
Kosher salt to taste
Freshly ground black pepper
   to taste
4 (12-inch) flour tortillas

> **TIP:** *Chorizo, the spicy sausage beloved in Spain, Portugal, and Latin America, is increasingly available in supermarkets. Chorizo is made differently in various nations, so taste around to find the one you like best.*

Melt the butter in a large nonstick sauté pan set over medium heat and swirl the pan to coat the surface. Add the chorizo and sauté it, stirring it frequently, for about 1 minute or until it is hot.

Add the eggs, cheese, salsa, scallions, salt, and pepper and cook the mixture, folding it gently with a spatula, for about 5 minutes, or until the eggs are thoroughly cooked. Remove it from the heat and keep it warm.

Place the tortillas on a microwave-safe plate and warm them in a microwave oven on medium power for 30 seconds. Place 1 tortilla on a work surface and spoon one-fourth of the egg mixture into the center. Fold the left and right edges in toward the center. Fold the edge closest to you toward the center; then roll the entire burrito away from you to seal it, with the seam on the bottom. (The eggs should soften the burrito enough so that it sticks together.) Cut the burrito in half on a diagonal. Keep it warm and repeat the process with the remaining 3 tortillas and the rest of the filling.

To serve, place 2 halves on each individual plate or cut the burritos into quarters and place them into a heated chafing dish for a buffet.

*Time for Brunch: This burrito is best made just before you plan to serve it. Have your ingredients prepped and ready to go; the cooking and assembly is quick and easy.*

# scrambled eggs and cheddar cheese on croissants

. . . . . . . . . . . . . . . . . . . . . . .

*makes 4 large or 12 petite croissant sandwiches*

*A Golden Pear Cafe favorite! This recipe can serve four as a main course or twelve as a buffet item for a larger brunch. Just vary the croissants' size: Use large croissants for a main course and the petite size for a buffet. Do buy the very best croissants you can find; forget the crescent-shaped, mass-produced bread that passes for croissants in some supermarkets and go for the real thing—flakey, buttery authentic French pastry. For a really over-the-top treat, add a few slices of crisp bacon or quickly sautéed Black Forest ham.*

Nonstick vegetable oil spray

12 large eggs

3 tablespoons heavy cream

2 tablespoons finely chopped fresh chives

2 teaspoons kosher salt

½ teaspoon freshly ground black pepper

4 large or 12 petite croissants

8 slices bacon or 4 slices Black Forest ham, optional

¼ stick (2 tablespoons) lightly salted butter, plus 1 tablespoon, optional, for cooking ham

1 cup grated sharp farmhouse Cheddar cheese (4 ounces)

6 fresh parsley sprigs, for garnish

6 fresh strawberries, hulled, washed, and patted dry, for garnish

1 pint fresh blueberries (1 cup), washed in a fine-mesh strainer and drained, for garnish

2 oranges, cut into rounds and then into half-moons, for garnish

> *TIP: Always buy good quality Cheddar and slice it by hand. I like to use Vermont Cheddar cheese because the cheese producers in that state, both large manufacturers and small artisan companies, routinely make such an excellent product. I also like New York Cheddars for the same reason, as well as some imports from England. Taste around to find a Cheddar you like; look for a tangy, satisfyingly sharp flavor.*

Preheat the oven to 350 degrees F. Spray a large sheet pan lightly with non-stick vegetable oil spray.

Crack the eggs into a large mixing bowl. Add the cream and whisk the mixture vigorously for 1 minute. Add the chives, salt, and pepper and whisk it gently for 30 seconds.

Cut the croissants in half and place them on a work surface close to the oven.

If you are adding bacon, cook it in a skillet over medium heat until it is golden and crispy. Drain it on paper towels. (Or line a microwave-safe plate with paper towels, place the bacon on top in a single layer, and microwave it on high power for 2 to 4 minutes or until it is golden and crispy. Drain it on fresh paper towels.) If you are adding ham, cook it with 1 tablespoon of butter in a skillet set over medium-high heat for 1 to 2 minutes or until it is lightly golden. If you are serving 12, cut each slice of bacon or ham into 3 pieces when it is cool enough to handle.

Melt 2 tablespoons of butter in a large nonstick sauté pan set over medium heat and swirl the pan to coat the surface. Increase the heat to high, add the egg mixture, and cook it, folding it gently with a rubber spatula, for 2 to 3 minutes or until it is cooked through but still soft. Remove the pan from the heat and, with a large serving spoon, place equal portions of egg onto the bottom half of each croissant. Top each with equal portions of Cheddar cheese. If you are adding bacon or ham, distribute it evenly among the sandwiches. Cover each sandwich with the top half of the croissant.

Place the croissant sandwiches onto the prepared sheet pan and warm them in the oven for 5 minutes; then transfer them to a large serving platter or chafing dish. Garnish them with parsley sprigs, fresh berries, and orange slices.

*Time for Brunch: These sandwiches are best made just before you plan to serve them; don't even try to save the leftovers, as they don't store well. Best just to gobble them up!*

# belgian waffles
# with all the fixings

*makes 4 large round waffles or 16 waffle wedges*

*When we bring out an order of Belgian waffles at any of our cafes, the people at the other tables invariably ooh and aah. It's a treat for the senses—a light, ethereal waffle topped with strawberries, blueberries, and bananas that perfumes the air with vanilla and cinnamon. It works equally well for a large group or an intimate brunch for four. Do serve only pure Vermont maple syrup—nothing else will do. If you don't have a good-quality round waffle iron, you can use this batter for pancakes and garnish them with the same toppings.*

2 large eggs

About ⅔ stick unsalted butter (⅓ cup), melted

1¾ cups whole milk

2 teaspoons pure vanilla extract

1¾ cups cake flour

1 tablespoon granulated sugar

1 tablespoon packed light brown sugar

2 teaspoons baking powder

½ teaspoon kosher salt

1 teaspoon ground cinnamon

Nonstick vegetable oil spray

3 bananas

12 medium fresh strawberries, hulled, washed, patted dry, and sliced

1 pint fresh blueberries (2 cups), washed in a fine-mesh strainer and drained

Pure Vermont maple syrup, for serving, optional

Whipped cream, for serving, optional

Fruit preserves, for serving, optional

*TIP: Most if not all waffle irons sold these days are nonstick, but they still need to be "seasoned" before you use them. To season your new iron, plug it in, spray it with nonstick vegetable oil spray, and let it sit that way for at least five to seven minutes. It probably will smoke—and that's okay. Then you really should make a few test waffles—and discard them—to get your waffle iron cookin', so to speak.*

Preheat the waffle iron for at least 5 minutes.

Meanwhile, crack the eggs into a mixing bowl. Add the melted butter, milk, and vanilla and whisk the ingredients vigorously for 30 seconds or until they are thoroughly combined.

Sift the cake flour into another large mixing bowl. Add the granulated and brown sugars, baking powder, salt, and cinnamon. Stir the ingredients to combine them; then form a 3-inch depression or "well" in the center of this flour mixture. Slowly pour the egg mixture into the well and whisk vigorously to combine the wet and dry ingredients, gradually moving more and more flour from the outer edge of the bowl into the center until it is completely absorbed and you have a loose batter.

Spray the heated waffle iron on both sides with the nonstick vegetable oil spray; close the lid and wait 5 seconds. Meanwhile, preheat the oven to 185 degrees F.

Open the waffle iron and, using a 1-cup measuring cup, scoop up a little less than a full cup of batter into the machine, moving the cup as you pour so that the batter covers the waffle grid completely. (Depending on the depth and size of your waffle iron, you might need a little more or less batter to fill it.)

Close the lid and bake the waffle for 3 to 4 minutes; then open the machine and test to see if the waffle is done. It should be golden brown, but if you like your waffles crispy, bake it for another 30 seconds.

While the waffle is cooking, spray an ovenproof casserole dish with nonstick vegetable oil spray. If you are going to serve buffet style, spray the bowl of your chafing dish also. When the waffle is done, remove it from the iron and trim any uneven edges. If you are serving 4 people, place the waffle into the prepared casserole dish, cover it with aluminum foil, and keep it warm in the oven. For a larger brunch, cut the waffle into 4 wedges before you put it into the casserole. Repeat the process with the remaining waffle batter to make 3 more waffles.

Just before you are ready to serve, peel the bananas and slice them into small rounds.

To serve, for 4 people, place a waffle on each plate and top each with equal portions of strawberries, blueberries, and bananas. For a larger brunch, place the waffle wedges into the prepared chafing dish and arrange the strawberries, blueberries, and bananas in bowls in front of it so guests can serve themselves. If you wish, serve the waffles with pure maple syrup, whipped cream, and/or preserves.

*Time for Brunch: Make your waffles up to 1 hour in advance, cover them and keep them warm in a 185-degree oven. Don't slice the bananas until just before you are ready to serve, or they will turn brown.*

# organic yogurt with banana, berries, and maple granola

*makes 6 servings*

The Golden Pear Cafe's granola is a healthy, delicious mix of organic oats, sunflower seeds, filberts, walnuts, and maple syrup. We always pair it with the Stonyfield brand of organic yogurt, which is widely available in supermarkets. You can use the granola and yogurt of your choice, but we like organic: It's not only that it's better for you; it usually tastes better, too. If you'd like to use this dish as a buffet item, serve the various ingredients in separate bowls and let your guests serve themselves. One caveat: If you do this on a buffet, omit the bananas, as they'll turn brown when exposed to the air.

24 ounces organic plain yogurt
  (3 cups)
1½ cups maple-flavored
  granola
2 medium bananas
¾ pint fresh blueberries (1½ cups),
  washed in a fine-mesh strainer
  and drained

¾ pint fresh strawberries
  (1½ cups), hulled, washed,
  patted dry, and sliced
¾ pint fresh blackberries (1½
  cups), washed in a fine-mesh
  strainer and drained
Pure maple syrup, optional
Sugar or other sweetener, optional

Spoon ½ cup yogurt each into 6 individual serving bowls. Add ¼ cup granola.
  Peel the bananas and slice them into rounds. Arrange about ¼ cup of banana slices on each bowl of granola. Top each with ¼ cup of blueberries, ¼ cup of strawberries, and ¼ cup of blackberries. If you wish, drizzle this dish with maple syrup or sprinkle it with the sweetener of your choice.

*Time for Brunch: For individual servings, prep your berries in advance, but cut the bananas just before serving, so they don't turn brown. Likewise, assemble the portions just prior to serving, so the granola retains its crunch.*

# oh-so-good oatmeal

. . . . . . . . . . . . . . . . . . . . . . . . . . . . . .

*makes 4 servings*

*Oatmeal for brunch? Why not? Especially when it's made with fresh, luscious fruit and hearty, flavorful rolled oats. Do use filtered water; the stuff from the tap can contain impurities that will give your oats an off taste. Don't slice the bananas until just before you're ready to serve, or they'll turn brown.*

6 cups water, preferably filtered

1 teaspoon kosher salt

3 cups rolled oats (not instant oatmeal)

1 pint fresh strawberries (2 cups), hulled, washed, patted dry, and sliced

1 pint fresh blueberries (2 cups), washed in a fine-mesh strainer and drained

2 small bananas

½ teaspoon ground cinnamon

4 teaspoons light brown sugar

Fresh cream or milk, for serving

Bring the water and salt to a boil in a saucepan set over high heat. Add the oats and reduce the heat to low. Cook the oatmeal, stirring it occasionally, for about 5 minutes or until it is softened and thoroughly cooked.

Pour the oatmeal into serving bowls. Top each with about ¼ cup of strawberries and ¼ cup of blueberries. Peel the bananas and slice them into rounds. Top each bowl with about ¼ cup of bananas. Sprinkle each with ⅛ teaspoon of cinnamon and 1 teaspoon of brown sugar. Serve the oatmeal with fresh cream or milk. Or, for a buffet, serve the oatmeal in a covered, heated soup tureen and put out the fruit and toppings in separate bowls so guests can add their own.

*Time for Brunch: Make this oatmeal just before you plan to serve it. If it is on the buffet for more than 30 minutes, add ¼ cup of warm water and stir the oatmeal to moisten it thoroughly.*

# apple crumb muffins

*makes 24 small muffins*

*These light, tender muffins are studded with chunks of sweet-tart apple that almost melt in your mouth—a treat for breakfast, coffee break, brunch (of course), or an anytime snack. We use cinnamon in both the topping and batter; it gives the muffins a heavenly aroma. Of course, you can have too much of a good thing, which is what happened one night when a new baker made these. We normally bake seventy-five at a time and use seven ounces of cinnamon in each batch, but one morning I noticed that something was wrong with the apple muffins. I called the baker at home and asked him how much cinnamon he had used. When he answered, "Seven pounds!" all I could do was laugh, haul the seventy-five muffins to the trash, and bake up some new ones. If you wish, substitute blueberries for the apples, but keep your eye on the cinnamon.*

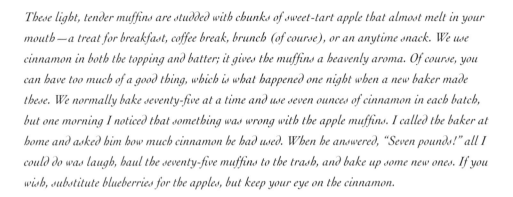

Nonstick vegetable oil spray

CRUMB TOPPING
2 cups all-purpose flour
¾ cup brown sugar
¾ cup granulated sugar
3 teaspoons ground cinnamon
½ teaspoon kosher salt
2 sticks (1 cup) cold unsalted
    butter, cut into ½-inch cubes

MUFFINS
2 sticks (1 cup) unsalted butter,
    softened
2 tablespoons canola oil

½ cup light brown sugar
½ cup granulated sugar
3 large eggs
2 teaspoons pure vanilla extract
2½ cups all-purpose flour
1 cup whole-wheat flour
1 tablespoon baking powder
1 teaspoon ground cinnamon
¼ teaspoon ground cloves
1 teaspoon kosher salt
1 cup whole milk
4 Granny Smith or Fuji apples,
    peeled, cored, and cut into
    ½ inch chunks (about (3 cups)

Preheat the oven to 350 degrees F. Spray a 24-cup muffin pan or 2 (12-cup) muffin pans with nonstick vegetable oil spray and line the muffin cups with paper liners.

*To prepare the crumb topping:* Pour the flour, brown sugar, granulated sugar, cinnamon, and salt into a bowl. Using an electric mixer set at low speed, mix the ingredients until they are combined. (If you have a KitchenAid stand mixer, use the flat paddle attachment.) Add the butter and mix it in at medium-low speed for about 5 minutes or until the mixture takes on the consistency of coarse crumbs. Transfer the crumb topping to a small bowl and set it aside.

*To prepare the muffin batter:* Wipe off the mixer blades or paddle. Combine the butter, canola oil, brown sugar, and granulated sugar in a separate bowl and mix them at low speed for 5 to 6 minutes or until the mixture is light and fluffy.

With a fork, gently beat the eggs and vanilla in a small bowl until they are combined. Pour the egg mixture into the butter mixture and mix them at low speed until they are blended. Stop the mixer occasionally and scrape down the side of the bowl and the beaters with a rubber spatula.

In a separate bowl, combine the all-purpose and whole-wheat flours, baking powder, cinnamon, cloves, and salt and stir them just to blend them. Add one-third of the flour mixture to the butter mixture and mix them at low speed until it is completely incorporated. Add ½ cup of milk and mix it in until it is completely incorporated. Increase the speed to medium and mix the batter for 30 seconds. Scrape down the side of the bowl after each addition as necessary. Add one-third of the flour mixture and mix it in at low speed until it is incorporated. Add the remaining ½ cup of milk and mix it in until it is completely incorporated. Increase the speed to medium and mix the batter for 30 seconds. Add the remaining one-third of the flour mixture and mix it in at low speed until it is completely incorporated. Increase the speed to medium and mix the batter for 30 seconds. Add the apple chunks and mix them in at low speed for 20 seconds, just to combine them into the batter.

Pour the batter into the muffin cups, filling them about three-fourths full. Working by the handful, gently squeeze the crumb topping and crumble it onto the filled muffin cups. Bake the muffins for 15 minutes; then rotate the pan 180 degrees to ensure even baking. Bake them for 20 minutes longer or until a toothpick inserted into the center of a muffin comes out clean. Place the muffin pans on a rack and cool the muffins in the pan for 5 to 10 minutes. Remove the muffins from the pan and cool them completely.

*Time for Brunch: Make these muffins in advance and freeze them in an airtight container for up to 2 months. Just before serving, warm the frozen muffins in a 325-degree oven for 5 minutes.*

# banana oatmeal muffins

*makes 24 small muffins*

*The bananas make these muffins extra moist, while the rolled oats give them a nice texture—and a healthy twist. We use real old-fashioned rolled oats to achieve the richest flavor.*

Nonstick vegetable oil spray

3 sticks (1½ cups) unsalted butter, softened

1½ cups granulated sugar

4 large eggs

1 tablespoon pure vanilla extract

5 cups all-purpose flour

2½ cups rolled oats (not instant)

2 tablespoons plus 1 teaspoon baking powder

1 tablespoon ground cinnamon

1½ teaspoons kosher salt

1½ cups whole milk

5 medium bananas

Preheat the oven to 350 degrees F. Spray a 24-cup muffin pan or 2 (12-cup) muffin pans with nonstick vegetable oil spray and line the muffin cups with paper liners.

Using an electric mixer set at medium speed, mix the butter and sugar in a large bowl for 5 to 6 minutes or until the mixture is light and fluffy. (If you have a KitchenAid stand mixer, use the flat paddle attachment.)

With a fork, gently beat the eggs and vanilla in a small bowl until they are combined. Pour the egg mixture into the butter mixture and mix them at low speed until they are blended. Stop the mixer occasionally and scrape down the side of the bowl and the beaters with a rubber spatula.

In a separate bowl, combine the flour, oats, baking powder, cinnamon, and salt and stir them just to blend them. Add one-third of the flour mixture to the butter mixture and mix them at low speed until it is completely incorporated. Add ¾ cup of milk and mix it in at low speed until it is completely incorporated. Increase the speed to medium and mix the batter for 30 seconds. Scrape down the side of the bowl after each addition as necessary. Add one-third of the flour mixture and mix it in at low speed until it is completely incorporated. Add the remaining ¾ cup of milk and mix it in at low speed until it is incorporated. Increase the speed to medium and mix the batter for 30 seconds. Add the remaining flour mixture and mix it in at low speed until it is completely incorporated. Increase the speed to medium and mix the batter for 30 seconds.

With a fork, mash the bananas lightly but do not puree them. Then, with the fork, fold the bananas into the batter. Pour the batter into the muffin cups, filling them very full. Bake the muffins for 20 minutes; then rotate the pan 180 degrees to ensure even baking. Bake them for 20 to 22 minutes longer or until a toothpick inserted into the center of a muffin comes out clean and the muffins are golden brown and slightly cracked on top. Place the muffin pan on a rack and cool the muffins in the pan for 5 to 10 minutes. Remove the muffins from the pan and cool them completely.

*Time for Brunch: Make these muffins in advance and freeze them in an airtight container for up to 2 months. Just before serving, warm the frozen muffins in a 325-degree oven for 5 minutes.*

# blueberry muffins

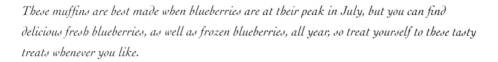

*makes 24 small muffins*

*These muffins are best made when blueberries are at their peak in July, but you can find delicious fresh blueberries, as well as frozen blueberries, all year, so treat yourself to these tasty treats whenever you like.*

Nonstick vegetable oil spray

3 sticks (1½ cups) unsalted butter, softened

1⅔ cups granulated sugar

4 large eggs

2¼ teaspoons pure vanilla extract

4½ cups all-purpose flour, plus ¼ cup for dusting

1⅓ cups whole-wheat flour

2 tablespoons plus ¼ teaspoon baking powder

1½ teaspoons kosher salt

1 pint whole milk

1¼ pints fresh blueberries (2½ cups), washed in a fine-mesh strainer and drained

2 tablespoons confectioners' sugar, optional

Preheat the oven to 375 degrees F. Spray a 24-cup muffin pan or 2 (12-cup) muffin pans with nonstick vegetable oil spray and line the muffin cups with paper liners.

Using an electric mixer set at medium speed, mix the butter and sugar in a large bowl for 5 to 6 minutes or until the mixture is light and fluffy. (If you have a KitchenAid stand mixer, use the flat paddle attachment.)

With a fork, gently beat the eggs and vanilla in a small bowl until they are combined. Pour the egg mixture into the butter mixture and mix them at low speed until they are blended. Stop the mixer occasionally and scrape down the side of the bowl and the beaters with a rubber spatula.

In a separate bowl, combine 4½ cups of all-purpose flour with the whole-wheat flour, baking powder, and salt and stir them just to blend them. Add one-third of the flour mixture to the butter mixture and mix them at low speed until it is completely incorporated. Add 1 cup of milk and mix it in at low speed until it is completely incorporated. Increase the speed to medium and mix the batter for 30 seconds. Scrape down the side of the bowl after each addition as necessary. Add one-third of the flour mixture and mix it in at low speed until it is completely incorporated. Add the remaining 1 cup of milk and mix it in at low speed until it is completely incorporated. Increase the speed to medium and mix the batter for 30 seconds. Add the remaining flour mixture and mix it in at low speed until it is completely incorporated. Increase the speed to medium and mix the batter for 30 seconds.

Place the blueberries into a bowl and sprinkle them with the remaining ¼ cup of flour. Toss them gently to coat them. Using a rubber spatula, fold the blueberries into the batter.

Pour the batter into the muffin cups, filling them very full. Bake the muffins for 20 minutes; then rotate the pan 180 degrees to ensure even baking. Bake them for 18 to 20 minutes longer or until a toothpick inserted into the center of a muffin comes out clean and the muffins are golden brown and slightly cracked on top. Place the muffin pan on a rack and cool the muffins in the pan for 5 to 10 minutes. Remove the muffins from the pan and cool them completely.

If you wish, use a small fine-mesh strainer to sprinkle confectioners' sugar over the tops of the muffins before serving.

*Time for Brunch: Make these muffins in advance and freeze them in an airtight container for up to 2 months. Just before serving, warm the frozen muffins in a 325-degree oven for 5 minutes.*

# corn muffins

. . . . . . . . . . . . . . . . . . . . . .

*makes 24 small muffins*

*For years people have commented on how good—and how different—our corn muffins are. I believe it's because we use coarse cornmeal, which gives the muffin a unique flavor and texture. The honey gives them a little something extra, too. I love to cut them in half, toast them, and spread them with butter and raspberry jam.*

Nonstick vegetable oil spray

1¼ sticks (1⅛ cups) unsalted butter, softened

¼ cup honey

⅔ cup granulated sugar

3 large eggs

3 cups all-purpose flour

1½ cups coarse cornmeal

2 tablespoons plus 2 teaspoons baking powder

1 teaspoon kosher salt

1½ cups whole milk

Preheat the oven to 375 degrees F. Spray a 24-cup muffin pan or 2 (12-cup) muffin pans with nonstick vegetable oil spray and line the muffin cups with paper liners.

Using an electric mixer set at medium speed, mix the butter, honey, and sugar in a large bowl for 5 to 6 minutes or until the mixture is light and fluffy. (If you have a KitchenAid stand mixer, use the flat paddle attachment.)

With a fork, gently beat the eggs in a small bowl. Pour them into the butter mixture and mix them in at low speed until they are incorporated. Stop the mixer occasionally and scrape down the side of the bowl and the beaters with a rubber spatula.

In a separate bowl, combine the flour, cornmeal, baking powder, and salt and stir them just to blend them. Add one-third of the flour mixture to the butter mixture and mix it in at low speed until it is completely incorporated. Add ¾ cup of milk and mix it in on low speed until it is completely incorporated. Increase the speed to medium and mix the batter for 30 seconds. Scrape down the side of the bowl after each addition as necessary. Add one-third of the flour mixture and mix it in at low speed until it is completely incorporated. Add the remaining ¾ cup of milk and mix it in at low speed until

. . . . . . . . . . . . . . . . . . . . . . . . . . . . . . . . . . . . . . . . . . . . . .

it is completely incorporated. Increase the speed to medium and mix the batter for 30 seconds. Add the remaining flour mixture and mix it in at low speed until it is completely incorporated. Increase the speed to medium and mix the batter for 1 minute.

Pour the batter into the muffin cups, filling them very full. (The batter will be fairly stiff, and you can fill the muffin cups ½ inch to ¾ inch above the pan at the center of each muffin.) Bake the muffins for 15 minutes; then rotate the pan 180 degrees to ensure even baking.

Bake them for 5 to 10 minutes longer or until a toothpick inserted into the center of a muffin comes out clean and the muffins are golden brown and slightly cracked on top. Place the muffin pan on a rack and cool the muffins in the pan for 5 to 10 minutes. Remove the muffins from the pan and cool them completely.

*Time for Brunch: Make these muffins in advance and freeze them in an airtight container for up to 2 months. Just before serving, warm the frozen muffins in a 325-degree oven for 5 minutes.*

# cranberry walnut muffins

*makes 24 small muffins*

*One Christmas Eve, I stopped by the Golden Pear in East Hampton to wish the staff a merry Christmas. When I walked in, it was clear that they were excited about something. "Jennifer Lopez is here!" they said in hushed tones. And there she was, sitting with her mother and sister. The cafe was almost empty, and they were quietly enjoying cappuccino and muffins. I don't usually ask for autographs, but I knew my daughters, Emily and Sarah, would never forgive me if I didn't at least try. J.Lo graciously said she would sign for me when she finished her coffee. Sure enough, when they were done, she wrote out a Christmas greeting for my two girls. Then, suddenly, the cafe filled up and the customers began to buzz that Jennifer Lopez was in the building. She and her party made a hasty exit, but that night my girls got an early Christmas present, one they still treasure. These Cranberry Walnut Muffins make a delightful brunch item for fall, when fresh cranberries are available, but you can also toss a bag of fresh cranberries into the freezer for a midwinter treat. Just defrost the berries before you start to bake.*

Nonstick vegetable oil spray

3 sticks (1½ cups) unsalted butter, softened

1⅔ cups granulated sugar

4 large eggs

2¼ teaspoons pure vanilla extract

4½ cups all-purpose flour

1⅓ cups whole-wheat flour

2 tablespoons plus 2 teaspoons baking powder

1½ teaspoons kosher salt

1½ cups whole milk

3½ cups fresh cranberries

1 cup shelled walnuts, chopped into small pieces

Preheat the oven to 375 degrees F. Spray a 24-cup muffin pan or 2 (12-cup) muffin pans with nonstick vegetable oil spray and line the muffin cups with paper liners.

Using an electric mixer set at medium speed, mix the butter and sugar in a large bowl for 5 to 6 minutes or until the mixture is light and fluffy. (If you have a KitchenAid stand mixer, use the flat paddle attachment.)

With a fork, gently beat the eggs and vanilla in a small bowl until they are combined. Pour the egg mixture into the butter mixture and mix them at low speed until they are blended. Stop the mixer occasionally and scrape down the side of the bowl and the beaters with a rubber spatula.

In a separate bowl, combine the all-purpose and whole-wheat flours, baking powder, and salt and stir them just to blend them. Add one-third of the flour mixture to the butter mixture and mix it in at low speed until it is completely incorporated. Add ¾ cup of milk and mix it in at low speed until it is completely incorporated. Increase the speed to medium and mix the batter for 30 seconds. Add the cranberries and walnuts and mix on low speed for 30 seconds until they're fully incorporated. Stop the mixer and scrape down the side of the bowl after each addition as necessary. Add one-third of the flour mixture and mix it in at low speed until it is completely incorporated. Add the remaining ¾ cup of milk and mix it in at low speed until it is completely incorporated. Increase the speed to medium and mix the batter for 30 seconds. Add the remaining flour mixture and mix it in at low speed until it is completely incorporated. Increase the speed to medium and mix the batter for 30 seconds.

Pour the batter into the muffin cups, filling them very full. Bake the muffins for 20 minutes; then rotate the pan 180 degrees to ensure even baking. Bake them for 20 to 22 minutes longer or until a toothpick inserted into the center of a muffin comes out clean and the muffins are golden brown and slightly cracked on top. Place the muffin pan on a rack and cool the muffins in the pan for 5 to 10 minutes. Remove the muffins from the pan and cool them completely.

*Time for Brunch: Make these muffins in advance and freeze them in an airtight container for up to 2 months. Just before serving, warm the frozen muffins in a 325-degree oven for 5 minutes.*

# pumpkin spice muffins

*makes 24 small muffins*

*We always begin baking these around October 1. They remind everyone—staff and customers alike—that the seasons are changing and Halloween and Thanksgiving are just around the corner. We bake them right through winter and into early spring. The canned pumpkin makes the muffins tender and moist. Don't bother with canned preseasoned pumpkin pie filling, because you'll add your own spices, which makes the muffins wonderfully aromatic. As a plus, they're high in vitamin A.*

Nonstick vegetable oil spray

3 sticks (1½ cups) unsalted butter, softened

1½ cups granulated sugar

4 large eggs

1 tablespoon pure vanilla extract

3 cups canned pumpkin (not pumpkin pie filling) (24 ounces)

3½ cups all-purpose flour, plus 1½ teaspoons for dusting

1½ teaspoons baking soda

1½ teaspoons baking powder

1 teaspoon kosher salt

1½ teaspoons ground cinnamon

¾ teaspoon grated nutmeg

⅛ teaspoon ground cloves

1 cup whole milk

1 cup moist raisins

> *TIP: If your raisins aren't moist when they come out of the box, soak them in warm water for five minutes and then drain them.*

Preheat the oven to 375 degrees F. Spray a 24-cup muffin pan or 2 (12-cup) muffin pans with nonstick vegetable oil spray and line the muffin cups with paper liners.

Using an electric mixer set at medium speed, mix the butter and sugar in a large bowl for 5 to 6 minutes or until the mixture is light and fluffy. (If you have a KitchenAid stand mixer, use the flat paddle attachment.)

With a fork, gently beat the eggs and vanilla in a small bowl until they are combined. Pour the egg mixture into the butter mixture and mix them at low speed until they are blended. Stop the mixer occasionally and scrape down the side of the bowl and the beaters with a rubber spatula. Add the pumpkin and mix it in until it is just blended.

In a separate bowl, combine the flour, baking soda, baking powder, salt, cinnamon, nutmeg, and cloves and stir them just to blend them. Add one-third of the flour mixture to the butter mixture and mix them at low speed until it is completely incorporated. Add ½ cup of milk and mix it in at low speed until it is completely incorporated. Increase the speed to medium and mix the batter for 30 seconds. Scrape down the side of the bowl after each addition as necessary. Add one-third of the flour mixture and mix it in at low speed until it is completely incorporated. Add the remaining ½ cup of milk and mix it in at low speed until it is completely incorporated. Increase the speed to medium and mix the batter for 30 seconds. Add the remaining flour mixture and mix it in at low speed until it is completely incorporated. Increase the speed to medium and mix the batter for 30 seconds.

Place the raisins into a bowl and sprinkle them with the remaining 1½ teaspoons of flour. Toss them gently to coat them. Using a rubber spatula, fold the raisins into the batter.

Pour the batter into the muffin cups, filling them very full. Bake the muffins for 20 minutes; then rotate the pan 180 degrees to ensure even baking. Bake them for 20 minutes longer or until a toothpick inserted into the center of a muffin comes out clean and the muffins are golden brown and slightly cracked on top. Place the muffin pan on a rack and cool the muffins in the pan for 5 to 10 minutes. Remove the muffins from the pan and cool them completely.

*Time for Brunch: Make these muffins in advance and freeze them in an airtight container for up to 2 months. Just before serving, warm the frozen muffins in a 325-degree oven for 5 minutes.*

# raisin scones

*makes 24 scones*

*We have been baking these scones from the day we opened. The recipe has never changed (because they're so good), and we have to bake them seven nights a week to keep up with the demand. They're not too sweet, just really delicious, and they're ideal for a quiet breakfast with the family or brunch for a crowd. Try them toasted and slathered with butter or, better yet, with authentic clotted cream and your favorite jam.*

Nonstick vegetable oil spray

7 cups all-purpose flour

1 cup granulated sugar

3 tablespoons baking powder

2½ teaspoons kosher salt

1¾ sticks (¾ cup plus 2 tablespoons) very cold unsalted butter, cut into small pieces

3¼ cups very cold half and half

2 cups raisins

1 egg yolk

Clotted cream, for serving, optional

Butter, for serving, optional

Jam, for serving, optional

> *TIP: For a "very British" brunch experience, serve your scones with clotted cream, a cross between butter and whipped cream or ice cream traditionally made by scalding un-pasteurized milk until a layer of cream rose to the top. At one time, clotted cream was a rarity in the United States due to its reliance on unpasteurized milk, but in recent years a jarred pasteurized version has become available. Now that we can enjoy it here, it's a treat not to be missed!*

Preheat the oven to 350 degrees F. Spray 2 (10 × 12-inch) baking sheets with nonstick vegetable oil spray and line them with parchment paper. Flour a work surface.

Using an electric mixer set at low speed, mix the flour, sugar, baking powder, and salt in a large bowl. (If you have a KitchenAid stand mixer, use the flat paddle attachment.) Add the butter and mix it in at low speed for 7 to 10 minutes or until the butter is chopped into very small pieces. Add 3 cups of half and half and mix it in just until the dough starts to pull away from the side of the bowl. Turn the dough out onto the prepared work surface.

Lightly knead the raisins into the dough. Roll the dough into a disk about 1½ inches high. Cut the disk with a 3½-inch round cookie cutter with either a fluted or straight edge. Cut each round in half and place them on the prepared baking sheet, evenly spaced.

Make an egg wash: Using a fork, gently beat the egg yolk with ¼ cup of half and half in a small bowl or cup. Using a pastry brush, brush the top of each scone with some egg wash. Bake the scones for 20 minutes; then rotate the pan 180 degrees to ensure even baking. Bake them for 15 to 20 minutes longer or until they are golden.

Remove the scones from the baking sheet and cool them on a wire rack. If you wish, serve them with clotted cream, butter, or your favorite jam.

*Time for Brunch: These scones are best when you bake them and serve them the same day. Freeze any leftovers in an airtight container for up to 2 months. You can reheat the frozen scones for 10 minutes in a 325-degree oven. It's not necessary to defrost them.*

# 3 · soups, chili, and stews

## The Hamptons in Winter

Years ago, when Labor Day came and the summer season officially ended, the Hamptons made its annual transformation from bustling cosmopolitan resort to sleepy oceanside community. It happened overnight. The fancy cars driving a bit too fast disappeared from the

◄ Golden Pear Gazpacho

streets, and many businesses—from hotels and restaurants to salons and gift shops—shuttered their windows and closed down altogether.

Now, with e-business and telecommuting and all the other advances in the way people conduct their professional lives, the Hamptons have become a year-round community. Businesses that used to close for the fall and winter are now open all year. Spending the winter holidays in the Hamptons has become the thing to do; it's fun to see our seaside villages decked out in holiday finery. These days, our winter visitors throw lots of fabulous holiday parties. The Golden Pear does a tremendous amount of holiday pie and cookie baking from Thanksgiving through New Year's. Then there's the "midwinter getaway," when people bundle up for walks along the snow-dusted beaches and warm up over lunch at the Golden Pear or dinner at a local restaurant. Of course, it's not like the summer—nothing is—but winter in the Hamptons is busier than it used to be.

Sometime in February, we start to see the prospective summer renters as they come out to preview their warm-weather digs. You can spot them right away; they're the ones with the real estate pages spread out in front of them as they sip their cafe mochas or warm up with our Butternut Squash with Apple Soup. You can't tell by looking, but it's a sure bet that several of the people seated quietly in our cafes will violate the local zoning ordinances by allowing too many guests to occupy their summer palaces (some will actually go home and set up Web sites to sign up housemates, known locally as house shares). Others will be visited by the local police for parties that last into the night. (It probably doesn't occur to my summer neighbors that I rise at 5:30 each morning to make sure their coffee and muffins are hot and fresh when they eventually make their way to brunch.) That's all to come in the crazy months of high season, though. In winter, the Hamptons are just busy enough.

# country chicken soup

*makes 2 quarts (6 to 8 servings)*

*Here's a modern twist on Grandma's chicken soup. Our secret: rosemary, which gives it an irresistible aroma, and zucchini and yellow squash, which add the fresh flavor of summer. You can poach your own chicken for this soup or use a store-bought roasted chicken or even leftover chicken. Soup might not be typical brunch fare, but when you think about it, it's an ideal brunch menu item for a cold winter's day—or a coolish fall or early spring morning. That's because you can make a big pot of soup ahead of time; a few days in the refrigerator will only improve the flavor of most soups, as the ingredients have extra time to mingle and merge flavors.*

*How do you serve soup to a crowd? You needn't hire an army of waiters for a sit-down affair (although you can if you want to). Coffee mugs with handles and a good supply of soup spoons make soup work on a buffet. Set out your soup in an attractive serving tureen on a warmer or in a chafing dish and let guests ladle some into their own mugs. We guarantee that some will step up to the buffet for more soup!*

2 teaspoons kosher salt

3 (4-ounce) boneless, skinless chicken breast cutlets, trimmed, or 2 cups chopped roasted dark and white chicken

1 tablespoon olive oil

½ medium onion, cut into ¼-inch cubes (about 1 cup)

1½ medium carrots, cut into ¼-inch cubes (about 1 cup)

2 large stalks celery, cut into ¼-inch cubes (about 1 cup)

½ small zucchini, cut into ¼-inch cubes (about ½ cup)

½ small yellow squash, cut into ¼-inch cubes (about ½ cup)

6 cups Golden Pear Chicken Stock (see page 155), or canned chicken stock

1½ teaspoon fresh rosemary leaves

½ teaspoon freshly ground black pepper

1 tablespoon chopped fresh parsley, for garnish

Warmed crusty French bread, for serving

If you are cooking the chicken yourself, bring 4 cups of water to a boil in a small stockpot set over high heat. Add 1 teaspoon of salt. Carefully place the chicken into the pot. Reduce the heat to medium-low and simmer the chicken for about 10 minutes or until it is cooked through and no longer pink. With a slotted spoon, transfer the chicken to a clean platter. Cover it and refrigerate it until it is cool.

Heat the olive oil in a large stockpot set over medium heat. Add the onions, carrots, and celery and sauté them, stirring them and shaking the pot, for about 5 minutes or until they begin to soften and the onions are translucent. Add the zucchini and yellow squash and sauté the mixture for 2 to 3 minutes.

Add the stock and bring the mixture to a boil; then reduce the heat to a simmer. Remove the chicken from the refrigerator and dice it into ¼-inch cubes. Add the chicken, the rosemary, the remaining 1 teaspoon of salt, and the pepper to the stockpot and simmer it for 15 minutes longer.

Ladle the soup into bowls and garnish it with fresh chopped parsley or pour it into a chafing dish or tureen for a buffet. Serve the soup hot with slices of warmed crusty French bread.

*Time for Brunch: Make this satisfying soup up to 4 days in advance and store it, covered, in the refrigerator. Reheat it just before serving. Freeze any leftovers in an airtight container for up to 3 months.*

# hamptons clam chowder

*makes 2½ quarts (10 to 12 servings)*

*When it comes to clam chowder, there are basically two kinds: the creamy New England style and the tomato-laden Manhattan version. We favor the former—and so do our customers, even though so many of them are New Yorkers! If you like shucking clams, by all means go ahead, but you can save time by buying fresh or frozen chopped clams from your fishmonger or your grocery's fish department.*

2 slices bacon, chopped

1 stick (½ cup) unsalted butter

1 small onion, diced (about ½ cup)

¾ medium carrot, diced (about ½ cup)

1 large stalk celery, diced (about ½ cup)

½ cup all-purpose flour

4 cups clam juice

½ cup sherry

1½ cups heavy cream

4 large red potatoes, chopped into ¾-inch chunks (about 2 cups).

6 large fresh chowder clams, diced (about 1½ cups)

1 tablespoon chopped fresh parsley

¼ teaspoon dried thyme

½ teaspoon kosher salt

Pinch of ground white pepper

> *TIP: Use a good-quality bottled clam juice that consists of clam juice and a little salt—no additives. It'll taste a whole lot better.*

Cook the bacon in a medium stockpot set over medium heat, stirring it occasionally, for 2 to 3 minutes or until it is browned but not too crisp. Do not drain it. Add the butter, reduce the heat to low, and cook it for about 2 minutes or until the butter is melted. Swirl the pan to coat the surface.

Add the onions, carrot, and celery, increase the heat to medium, and sauté the vegetables, stirring them and shaking the pan, for about 5 minutes or until they are softened and the onions are translucent. Make a roux: Slowly whisk the flour into the vegetable mixture. Reduce the heat to low and cook the mixture, stirring it constantly, for about 2 to 3 minutes or until the flour is thoroughly dissolved and the roux is golden blond in color and will coat the back of a spoon. Be careful not to let it burn.

In a separate saucepan, bring the clam juice and sherry to a boil over medium-high heat. Reduce the heat to medium and simmer the mixture for 3 minutes. Then slowly add it to the roux and whisk it in thoroughly.

Slowly whisk in the cream.

Place the potatoes in a separate saucepan, add enough water to cover them, and set the pan over high heat. Bring them to a boil and boil them for 3 minutes. Strain the potatoes and add them to the chowder mixture.

Add the clams, parsley, thyme, salt, and white pepper. Stir the chowder gently over medium heat and simmer it, stirring it frequently, for 30 minutes. Taste it and season it again with salt and pepper if necessary.

Ladle the chowder into soup bowls or pour it into a chafing dish or tureen for a buffet. Serve it hot.

*Time for Brunch: Make this chowder up to 2 days in advance and refrigerate it, covered. Reheat it just before serving. Freeze any leftovers in an airtight container for up to 1 month.*

# butternut squash and apple soup

*makes 3 quarts (6 to 8 servings)*

*Years ago this was an autumn treat we shared mostly with the locals. Now that the Hamptons are a year-round destination, locals and guests alike enjoy the flavors of the late harvest in this savory soup. It's not one of our easiest recipes—peeling and chopping the thick-skinned butternut squash requires a sharp chef's knife and good hand strength—but it's definitely worth the effort.*

5 tablespoons unsalted butter

2 leeks, washed well and coarsely chopped (about 1½ cups)

2 large stalks celery, cut into large chunks (about 1 cup)

8 cups Golden Pear Chicken Stock (see page 155), or canned chicken stock

2 medium butternut squash, peeled and cut into large chunks (6 cups)

1 large apple, peeled, cored, and chopped into small chunks (about 1 cup)

1 cup heavy cream

¼ teaspoon dried thyme

½ teaspoon kosher salt

Pinch of ground white pepper

Freshly chopped thyme leaves, for garnish

Sour cream, for garnish

> *TIP: If you've never cleaned leeks before, you should know that they often contain significant amounts of sand and soil between their onion-like layers. Before you chop, slice the leek lengthwise, stopping just before the root, then rotate the leek and slice it lengthwise again. Hold the leek by the root end and wash it very well under running water, separating the layers to be sure you've washed out all the dirt.*

Melt 3 tablespoons of butter in a medium stockpot set over medium heat and swirl the pot to coat the surface. Add the leeks and celery and sauté them, stirring them and shaking the pan, for about 5 minutes or until they are softened but not browned. Add the chicken stock and bring it to a simmer. Add the squash and reduce the heat to medium-low. Simmer it for 20 minutes or until the squash is soft enough to be pierced easily with a fork.

Meanwhile, melt 2 tablespoons of butter in a saucepan set over medium heat and swirl the pan to coat the surface. Add the diced apple and sauté it, stirring, for about 5 minutes or until it is softened. Remove the pan from the heat and set it aside.

Transfer the vegetables to a food processor fitted with a metal blade or a blender and puree them until they are smooth. Work in batches if necessary. Transfer the mixture back to the stockpot and set it over medium heat. Slowly whisk the cream into the soup.

Add the sautéed apple and the thyme, salt, and white pepper. Stir the soup gently until all the ingredients are blended.

Ladle the soup into bowls or pour it into a chafing dish or tureen for a buffet. If you wish, garnish each serving with a sprinkling of chopped fresh thyme leaves and/or a dollop of sour cream. Serve the soup hot.

*Time for Brunch: Make this soup up to 4 days in advance and refrigerate it, covered. Reheat just before serving. Freeze any leftovers in an airtight container for up to 2 months.*

# golden pear gazpacho

*makes 3 quarts (10 to 12 servings)*

*Yes, most of the time we associate soup with a hot meal served in colder weather, but here's a soup that's an exception to the rule. If you need more than lemonade to refresh you on a hot summer day, this chilled gazpacho, infused with zesty fresh lime juice, will fit the bill. Use the freshest produce you can find. If you have tomatoes fresh from the garden or the farmers' market, by all means use them. Reduce or omit the hot sauce if you must, but we think it adds a pleasant kick.*

9 medium-large garden, vine-ripened, or plum tomatoes, cored, cut in half, and seeded

2 medium cucumbers, peeled, seeded, and cut into 1-inch chunks (about 3 cups)

1 large green bell pepper, seeded and cut into 1-inch chunks (about 2 cups)

1 large red bell pepper, seeded and cut into 1-inch chunks (about 2 cups)

1 yellow bell pepper, seeded and cut into 1-inch chunks (about 2 cups)

1 small yellow onion, cut into large chunks (about ½ cup)

2 medium cloves garlic, minced

½ cup finely chopped fresh cilantro

Juice of 4 limes (about ½ cup)

¾ cup red wine vinegar

½ cup extra-virgin olive oil

4 cups canned tomato juice

½ teaspoon hot pepper sauce such as Tabasco, or to taste

2 teaspoons kosher salt

1 teaspoon freshly ground black pepper

2 limes, sliced, for garnish

Place the tomatoes into a food processor fitted with a metal blade and quickly pulse them 6 or 7 times or until they are chopped into ¼-inch chunks. Transfer them to a large glass or stainless steel bowl. Repeat the process with the cucumbers, again with the bell peppers, and again with the onions, working in 3 separate batches and adding each batch to the tomatoes.

Add the garlic, cilantro, lime juice, wine vinegar, olive oil, tomato juice, and hot sauce to the tomato mixture and season it with salt and pepper. Toss it to combine the ingredients. Cover the bowl with plastic wrap and refrigerate it for at least 1 hour.

Just before serving, taste the gazpacho and season it with salt and pepper if necessary. Serve the soup chilled in large mugs, garnished with lime slices.

*Time for Brunch: Make this zesty soup up to 3 days in advance and store it, covered, in the refrigerator. Don't try to freeze it; the veggies will get mushy.*

# texas turkey chili

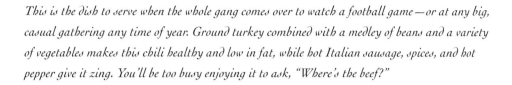

*makes 4 quarts (14 to 16 servings)*

*This is the dish to serve when the whole gang comes over to watch a football game—or at any big, casual gathering any time of year. Ground turkey combined with a medley of beans and a variety of vegetables makes this chili healthy and low in fat, while hot Italian sausage, spices, and hot pepper give it zing. You'll be too busy enjoying it to ask, "Where's the beef?"*

5 links hot Italian sausage

2 tablespoons olive oil

1 to 1½ pounds low-fat ground turkey

2 cups Golden Pear Vegetable Stock (see page 157), or canned vegetable stock

2 medium onions, cut into ¼-inch cubes (about 4 cups)

2 medium cloves garlic, diced

2 large green bell peppers, seeds and ribs removed and cut into ¼-inch cubes (about 3 cups)

1 jalapeño pepper, seeds and ribs removed, and diced

2 (28-ounce) cans whole plum tomatoes

1 (28-ounce) can crushed tomatoes

3½ cups cold water, preferably filtered

1 (15.5-ounce) can dark kidney beans, rinsed and drained (about 2 cups)

1 (15.5-ounce) can black beans, rinsed and drained (about 2 cups)

1 (15.5-ounce) can garbanzo beans, rinsed and drained (about 2 cups)

1 (15.5-ounce) can cannellini beans, rinsed and drained (about 2 cups)

½ teaspoon hot pepper sauce such as Tabasco

3 tablespoons chili powder

1 tablespoon ground cumin

2 tablespoons kosher salt

1 tablespoon freshly ground black pepper

Grated Cheddar cheese, for serving

Grated Monterey Jack cheese, for serving

6 ripe medium plum tomatoes, diced, for serving

2 medium onions, diced, for serving

6 scallions, chopped, for serving

Preheat the oven to 375 degrees F. and line a baking sheet with parchment paper. Place the sausage links on the baking sheet and place it on the center rack of the oven. Bake the sausage for 30 minutes or until an instant-read thermometer inserted into it reads 160 degrees F. Set it aside to cool.

Heat the olive oil in a large stockpot set over medium heat and swirl the pot to coat the surface. Add the turkey and cook it, stirring it frequently and breaking up any clumps of meat with a wooden spoon, for about 10 minutes. When the meat is browned, stir in 1 cup of vegetable stock, scraping up any browned bits of turkey from the bottom of the pot.

Add the onions and sauté them, stirring them and shaking the pan, for about 3 minutes. Add the garlic and cook the mixture, stirring, for 3 minutes. Add the green and jalapeño peppers and cook them, stirring the mixture, over medium heat until the peppers are softened.

Pour the plum tomatoes into a large bowl. Squeeze them with your hands to break them into large chunks. Add them and the crushed tomatoes to the pot and stir the mixture. Add the cold water and stir it again.

Stir in the kidney, black, garbanzo, and cannellini beans and the remaining 1 cup of vegetable stock. Add the hot sauce, chili powder, cumin, salt, and black pepper and stir the chili to blend all the ingredients well. Slice the sausage links into thin rounds, add them to the chili, and stir it to combine the ingredients thoroughly. Bring the chili to a simmer, reduce the heat to low, and cook it for 1 hour, stirring it every 5 to 7 minutes.

Ladle the chili into large deep bowls or crocks. Top it with grated Cheddar and/or Monterey Jack cheese, diced tomato, onions, and scallions.

*Time for Brunch: Make this chili up to 4 days in advance and refrigerate it, covered. Reheat it just before serving. Freeze any leftovers in an airtight container for up to 3 months.*

# rosemary chicken stew

*makes about 4½ quarts (12 to 15 servings)*

*This recipe is a favorite Golden Pear lunch entrée during the winter months. It has a creamy sauce with lots of chunky chicken and vegetables. A hint of rosemary gives it a fragrant quality that sets it apart from all others.*

3 pounds boneless, skinless chicken breast cutlets, trimmed and cut into bite-sized pieces

¾ stick (6 tablespoons) unsalted butter

6 tablespoons all-purpose flour

1½ medium onions, chopped into ½-inch pieces (about 3 cups)

3 medium carrots, cut into ½-inch cubes (about 2 cups)

4 large stalks celery, cut into ½-inch cubes (about 2 cups)

1 pound medium white mushrooms, washed and quartered

4 cups Golden Pear Chicken Stock (see page 155), or canned chicken stock

Leaves of 1 sprig fresh rosemary

Kosher salt to taste

Freshly ground black pepper, or to taste

1 pound Yukon Gold potatoes, cut into bite-sized pieces

1 pound frozen peas

¼ cup chopped fresh parsley

Warmed fresh bread, for serving

Bring 4 quarts of water to a boil in a 6-quart stockpot and add a pinch of salt. Carefully place the chicken into the boiling water. Cook it for 10 to 15 minutes or until the meat is cooked through and no longer pink. Using a slotted spoon, transfer the chicken to a bowl. Reserve 3 cups of the poaching liquid.

Make a roux: Melt ½ stick of butter in a small saucepan set over low heat. Add the flour and cook the mixture, stirring it constantly, for about 2 minutes or until the flour is thoroughly dissolved and the roux is golden blond in color. Be careful not to let it burn. Whisk in 1 cup of the reserved poaching liquid. Remove it from the heat and keep it warm.

Rinse and dry the stockpot and set it over medium-high heat. Add 2 tablespoons of butter and heat it until it is melted. Add the onions and sauté them, stirring them and shaking the pan, for 3 minutes or until they are soft and translucent. Add the carrots and celery and cook the vegetables, stirring them, for 3 minutes. Add the mushrooms and cook the mixture, stirring it occasionally, until they are softened.

Add the chicken stock, 2 cups of the reserved poaching liquid, and the rosemary leaves, salt, and pepper. Bring it to a boil, reduce the heat to medium-low, and whisk in the roux. Add the potatoes and chicken and simmer the stew for 10 to 15 minutes or until the potatoes are tender. Add the peas and parsley and cook it for 2 to 5 minutes or until the peas are heated through. Serve the stew with warm fresh-baked bread.

*Time for Brunch: Make this stew up to 3 days in advance and refrigerate it, covered. Just before serving, heat it in a large saucepan on the stovetop over medium heat, stirring it frequently, for 20 minutes. Freeze any leftovers in an airtight container for up to 2 months.*

# southampton shellfish stew

*makes 10 to 12 servings*

. . . . . . . . . . . . . . . . . . . . . . . . . .

*The great thing about this stew is that you can eat it year-round. It's as good on a cold winter night as it is at a summer clambake at the beach. Chock full of fresh clams, scallops, and shrimp, it's divine. Buy freshly made fish stock from your local fishmonger or scout out a bottled (not canned) clam juice that is made without chemical additives.*

¼ cup olive oil

1 large sweet white onion such as Vidalia, cut into 1-inch pieces (about 3 cups)

3 medium carrots, cut into ½-inch pieces (about 2 cups)

4 large stalks celery, cut into ½-inch pieces (about 2 cups)

3 medium cloves garlic, coarsely chopped

2 medium bulbs fennel, trimmed, cored, and cut into 1-inch pieces (about 3 cups)

5 medium Yukon Gold potatoes, peeled and cut into ¾-inch pieces (about 4 cups)

1 (28-ounce) can peeled tomatoes

1 (28-ounce) can crushed tomatoes

3 cups fish stock or clam juice

1 cup dry sherry

2 tablespoons fresh thyme leaves

1 tablespoon kosher salt

1 teaspoon freshly ground black pepper

36 fresh littleneck clams in the shell, scrubbed clean

1½ pounds sea scallops (about 3 cups)

24 jumbo (U-15) shrimp, peeled and deveined, tail on

12 large fresh basil leaves, sliced in chiffonade (see page 117)

Warmed crusty French bread, for serving

> *TIP: To trim fennel, cut and discard the feathery leaves and all but about 1 inch of the stalky "fingers" attached to the bulb. Next, cut a V-shape into the bulb's root end and remove the core. Then slice the remaining bulb into whatever size you wish.*

In a large (at least 12-quart) stockpot, heat the olive oil over medium-high heat for 1 minute. Add the onions and sauté them, stirring them frequently, for 5 minutes or until they are soft and translucent. Add the carrots, celery, garlic, and fennel and sauté the mixture, stirring it frequently, for 5 minutes or until the vegetables are softened. Add the potatoes and cook it, stirring, for 5 minutes longer.

Meanwhile, squeeze the peeled tomatoes a bit with your hands to break them up. Reduce the heat under the stockpot to medium and add the crushed tomatoes. Cover the pot and simmer the mixture, stirring it frequently, for 10 minutes.

Add the fish stock and sherry, reduce the heat to medium-low, cover the pot, and simmer the mixture, stirring it occasionally, for 30 minutes.

Stir in the thyme, salt, and pepper. Check the potatoes; they should be tender and easy to pierce with a fork. Add the clams, spooning them gently onto the surface of the stew. Cover the pot and simmer the stew for 5 minutes. When the clams just begin to open, add the scallops and shrimp, stir the stew gently, cover the pot, and simmer it for 5 minutes longer. Gently stir in the basil.

When the clams are completely open, the stew is finished. Ladle it immediately into large bowls and serve it hot with warmed crusty French bread.

*Time for Brunch: You can prep the vegetables ahead of time, but this dish is best cooked just before serving. You can refrigerate any leftover stew for up to 4 days, but don't try to freeze it.*

# new england beef stew

*This soul-satisfying stew is just the thing when the weather turns chilly, either for Sunday brunch or Sunday supper. Whatever time of day you serve it, you'll be delighted with the healthy combination of lean stew beef, hearty vegetables, and earthy potatoes. This recipe begins on the stovetop, but you can finish it there or you can braise it (that is, cook it in the oven in a little liquid). If you choose the latter, make sure your cooking vessel is ovenproof.*

¼ cup olive oil

4 to 5 strips good-quality bacon

1 cup all-purpose flour

3 pounds cubed boneless beef stew meat

1 pound white mushrooms, quartered

1 cup dry red wine

7 cups canned beef broth

1 (6-ounce) can tomato paste (¾ cup)

7 teaspoons kosher salt

1 teaspoon freshly ground black pepper

Leaves of 1 sprig fresh rosemary

1 medium onion, cut into 1-inch chunks (2 cups)

3 medium carrots, cut into 1-inch pieces (about 2 cups)

4 large stalks celery, cut into ½-inch pieces (about 2 cups)

8 medium Yukon Gold or red potatoes, peeled and cut into 1- to 1¼-inch chunks (about 3 cups)

8 ounces frozen peas (about 1½ cups), rinsed quickly under warm water

¼ cup finely chopped fresh parsley

Fresh parsley sprigs, for garnish

Warmed crusty French bread, for serving

> ✑ **TIP:** When you brown meat in oil or other fat, it caramelizes, releasing its natural flavors. Some tiny bits of meat and caramelized juices will get stuck to the pan. These aren't burned; in fact, they're precious morsels of flavor! Use them to best advantage by deglazing the pan (by adding stock or wine to it) and scraping the bits off with a wooden spoon. The result will be the beginning of a luscious sauce for whatever you're cooking.

If you will be finishing the stew in the oven, preheat it to 350 degrees F. Heat the oil in a large stockpot or Dutch oven set over medium-high heat until it sizzles and swirl the pot to coat the surface. Add the bacon and cook it, turning it occasionally, for 4 to 5 minutes or until it just begins to brown.

While the bacon is cooking, pour 1 cup of flour into a medium bowl. Add the beef and toss it to coat it lightly on all sides, tapping off any excess. When the bacon starts to brown, add the beef to the pot and sauté it, stirring and turning it frequently, for about 5 minutes or until it is browned on all sides. Some meat might stick to the pan, but keep stirring and be careful not to let it burn. Add the mushrooms and cook the mixture until they are just barely softened.

Add the red wine, reduce the heat to medium, and cook the mixture, scraping the bottom of the stockpot with a wooden spoon to loosen any bits of browned meat, for 2 minutes. Add the beef broth, the tomato paste, 4 teaspoons of salt, and the pepper. Remove the leaves from the rosemary sprig and add them to the pot. If you are going to finish the stew on the stove, reduce the heat to medium-low, cover the pot, and simmer it, stirring it occasionally, for 1½ to 1¾ hours or until the beef is tender. If you are going to finish it in the oven, cover the pot, place it in the oven, and braise the stew, stirring it once or twice, for 1½ to 1¾ hours or until the beef is tender.

Meanwhile, place the onions, carrots, celery, and potatoes in a large saucepan and add enough cold water to cover them by 1 inch. Add the remaining 3 teaspoons of salt and bring the mixture to a boil over medium-high heat. Reduce the heat to medium-low and simmer the vegetables for 20 to 25 minutes or until they are just tender. Drain them in a colander and rinse them with cold water for about 30 seconds. Drain them again. Carefully spoon the cooked vegetables and the peas into the stew and cook or braise it for 20 minutes longer.

To serve the stew, ladle equal portions into serving bowls. Sprinkle each serving with chopped parsley and garnish it with parsley sprigs. Serve this dish hot with warmed crusty French bread.

*Time for Brunch: Make this stew up to 3 days in advance and store it, covered, in the refrigerator. Just before serving, heat it in a large saucepan on the stovetop over medium heat, stirring it frequently, for 20 minutes. Freeze any leftovers in an airtight container for up to 2 months.*

# 4 · salads, sandwiches, and wraps

The pace of life here changes dramatically on Memorial Day weekend. Thereafter, the lines at every business establishment are longer, the parking lots more crowded. Reservations, whether at restaurants or hair salons, are harder to come by. The village streets are packed with ex-

◄ Roasted Turkey, Brie with Herbs, and Honey Mustard Wraps

pensive cars, and you start to notice that the clothes people wear are much lighter and, well, a whole lot sexier.

You never quite know who it is ordering that sandwich of Black Forest Ham and Farmhouse Cheddar or Cajun Flank Steak with Roasted Tomatoes. It could be a guy who has a house share with sixteen other refugees from the hot streets of New York—or it could be the millionaire next door. (You'll get a clue as to who's the millionaire when he takes out a little black American Express card to pay for it—I'm pretty sure you have to spend upwards of $100K per year to get one.)

On the other hand, the person ordering that Grilled Vegetable and Fresh Mozzarella Wrap could be a movie or TV star. One day a few years ago, I was standing at the bakery station in the Golden Pear Cafe in Southampton. The usual crowd was there: a few locals in for morning coffee, pairs and three-somes of singles checking each other out while waiting for panini, and families loading up their baskets with lunch and snacks for a day at the beach. I looked over at the coffee bar and saw a tall, attractive woman pouring coffee. She looked up at me with those beautiful dark eyes, and I realized it was Brooke Shields. It sounds like a cliché, but she's even taller and prettier in real life. I think my heart actually skipped a beat. When something like that happens on an otherwise routine morning, you know it's summer in the Hamptons.

# balsamic grilled chicken salad

*makes 4 to 6 servings*

*This zesty chicken salad is full of contrasting colors, textures, and aromas—and you won't believe how easy the marinade and dressing are to make. When you taste this dish, you'll swear it's got to be more complicated. If you're entertaining a bigger crowd, just double or even triple the quantities. We also use this salad as the basis for our famous East Hampton Sandwich. Cut a whole-grain pita bread in half to make two pockets and scoop a healthy portion of the salad into each. Garnish it with fresh alfalfa sprouts and sliced tomato. It's a great "easy grab" for brunch platters.*

1 tablespoon extra-virgin olive oil

¼ cup balsamic vinegar

3 (4-ounce) boneless, skinless chicken breast cutlets, trimmed

1 medium zucchini, cut in half, each half sliced lengthwise, and cut diagonally into chunks (about 1 cup)

1 medium yellow squash, cut in half, each half sliced lengthwise, and cut diagonally into chunks (about 1 cup)

2 large stalks celery, cut in half, each half sliced lengthwise, and cut diagonally into chunks (about 1 cup)

½ cup drained, sliced bottled roasted red peppers

⅓ cup very thinly sliced fresh basil leaves

½ cup Balsamic Vinaigrette (see page 158)

1 tablespoon kosher salt

½ teaspoon freshly ground black pepper

½ head green leaf lettuce, leaves separated, trimmed, washed, and dried, or 1 small (7- to 10-ounce) bag baby salad greens, washed and dried

8 to 12 small fresh basil leaves, for garnish

To prepare the chicken, make a marinade by whisking the olive oil and balsamic vinegar in a shallow glass or stainless steel baking dish. Place the chicken into the dish in a single layer and turn it to coat it thoroughly. Cover it and refrigerate it for at least 2 hours or up to 24 hours.

Ten minutes before you plan to grill the chicken, remove it from the refrigerator. Prepare a charcoal fire or preheat a gas grill to medium. Place the chicken on the grill in a single layer and discard any remaining marinade. Grill the chicken for 3 to 4 minutes per side, turning it frequently, until it is no longer pink, the juices run clear, and an instant-read thermometer inserted into the thickest part of the breast reads 160 degrees F. Transfer the chicken to a clean plate, cover it, and refrigerate it for 20 to 30 minutes or until it is cool.

Meanwhile, place the zucchini, yellow squash, celery, and roasted red peppers into a large salad bowl. Add the basil and toss the salad gently until all the ingredients are well blended.

When the chicken has cooled, slice it on an angle across the grain into strips. Add the strips to the salad bowl. If you are not serving the salad immediately, cover and refrigerate it for up to 1 hour.

When you are ready to serve, pour the vinaigrette over the chicken salad and toss it gently. Season the salad with salt and pepper and toss it gently again. Line a large serving platter with lettuce and arrange the grilled chicken salad over it. Garnish it with basil leaves.

*Time for Brunch: Make the dressing up to 3 days in advance and store it, covered, in the refrigerator. Stir it well before using it. Allow at least 1 hour and up to 24 hours for marinating the chicken. Grill the chicken up to 2 days in advance. If you grill it the day you're serving it, be sure to allow for the cooling time. Assemble the salad up to 1 hour before you plan to serve it, but don't add the dressing until immediately before serving.*

# citrus veggie tuna salad

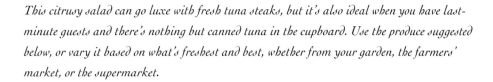

*makes 6 servings*

*This citrusy salad can go luxe with fresh tuna steaks, but it's also ideal when you have last-minute guests and there's nothing but canned tuna in the cupboard. Use the produce suggested below, or vary it based on what's freshest and best, whether from your garden, the farmers' market, or the supermarket.*

2 (8- to 10-ounce) tuna steaks, or 4 (6-ounce) cans solid white tuna packed in water, drained

Canola oil for brushing

1 teaspoon kosher salt, or more to taste

1 teaspoon freshly ground black pepper, or more to taste

¾ medium carrot, diced (about ½ cup)

1 large stalk celery, diced (about ½ cup)

1 small cucumber, peeled, seeded, and diced (about 1 cup)

1 small zucchini, diced (about 1 cup)

1 small yellow squash, diced (about 1 cup)

1½ cups Citrus Vinaigrette (see page 159)

Fresh lemon juice to taste, optional

2 heads Bibb lettuce, leaves separated, trimmed, washed, and dried

Fresh herb sprigs such as parsley, thyme, or oregano, for garnish

> *TIP: When you are cooking fish, poultry, or meat, never place the cooked food back on the platter, cutting board, or container that held it when it was raw. If you do, you risk contaminating it with foodborne bacteria from raw juices. (Bacteria on the food itself will have been killed by the heat of cooking.) Be safe: Always use a clean plate to hold cooked food.*

If you are using fresh tuna steaks, prepare a charcoal fire or preheat a gas grill to high. Brush the tuna steaks with canola oil and season both sides with salt and pepper. Grill the steaks for 4 minutes per side, transfer them to a clean platter, cover them, and refrigerate them for at least 1 hour until you are ready to assemble the salad.

Break the cooled tuna into pieces and place them into a large bowl. If you are using canned tuna, drain it well and spoon it into a large bowl. Add the carrots, celery, cucumbers, zucchini, and yellow squash. Mix all the ingredients gently with a rubber spatula until they are well blended. If you are not going to serve the salad immediately, cover it and refrigerate it for up to 1 hour.

Just before serving, pour the vinaigrette over the tuna salad and toss it gently with a rubber spatula until the salad is thoroughly coated. Taste it and season it with more salt, pepper, and/or lemon juice if necessary.

To serve, line a large serving bowl or platter with lettuce leaves and mound the tuna salad over the lettuce. Arrange the tomatoes around the perimeter of the dish. Garnish it with fresh herb sprigs.

*Time for Brunch: Make the vinaigrette up to 3 days in advance and store it, covered, in the refrigerator. Stir it well before using it. You can grill the tuna up to 1 day in advance and refrigerate it, covered. Mix the salad up to 1 hour in advance, but toss it with the vinaigrette and assemble the platter just before serving.*

# classic cobb salad

*makes 6 to 8 servings*

*Well, OK, maybe the traditional Cobb salad dressing wasn't made with balsamic vinegar and Dijon mustard or our secret ingredient, soy sauce—but you can't deny that our updates make a darn good salad. I like it best when the chicken is warm off the grill, but if you're serving a crowd and cooking in advance, you can refrigerate it until it's time to assemble the salad. It's darn good cold, too.*

### GOLDEN PEAR COBB DRESSING

¼ cup plus 2 tablespoons extra-virgin olive oil

2 tablespoons balsamic vinegar

1 tablespoon water

½ teaspoon soy sauce

1 teaspoon honey

½ teaspoon Dijon mustard

1 medium clove garlic, chopped

Kosher salt to taste

Freshly ground black pepper to taste

### COBB SALAD

1 tablespoon olive oil

¼ cup balsamic vinegar

4 (4-ounce) boneless, skinless chicken breast cutlets, trimmed

½ pound bacon

2 avocados

Juice of ½ lemon (about 1 tablespoon)

3 medium hearts of romaine lettuce, leaves separated, trimmed, washed, dried, and sliced lengthwise into quarters and then into 1-inch strips

1 medium head Bibb lettuce, leaves separated, trimmed, washed, dried, and torn into small pieces

8 medium baby bella mushrooms, trimmed and thinly sliced

10 to 12 grape tomatoes

1½ cups crumbled blue cheese (4 ounces)

Kosher salt to taste

Freshly ground black pepper to taste

*To prepare the dressing:* Whisk the extra-virgin olive oil, balsamic vinegar, water, soy sauce, honey, Dijon mustard, and garlic in a glass or stainless steel bowl and season the dressing with salt and pepper. Cover it and refrigerate it until you are ready to serve the salad.

*To prepare the chicken:* Make a marinade by whisking the olive oil and balsamic vinegar in a shallow glass or stainless steel baking dish. Place the chicken into the dish in a single layer and turn it with tongs to coat it thoroughly. Cover it and refrigerate it for at least 2 hours or up to 24 hours.

When you are ready to make the salad, preheat the oven to 350 degrees F. Place the bacon on a baking sheet in a single layer and bake it for about 10 minutes or until it is crispy. Carefully transfer the bacon to a plate lined with paper towels and drain it. (Or line a microwave-safe plate with paper towels, place the bacon on top in a single layer, and microwave it on high power for 2 to 4 minutes or until it is golden and crispy. Drain it on fresh paper towels.) When the bacon is cool enough to handle, chop it into bits and set it aside.

Ten minutes before you plan to grill the chicken, remove it from the refrigerator. Prepare a charcoal fire or preheat a gas grill to medium. Place the chicken on the grill in a single layer and discard any remaining marinade. Grill the chicken for 3 to 4 minutes per side, turning it frequently, until it is no longer pink, the juices run clear, and an instant-read thermometer inserted into the thickest part of the breast reads 160 degrees F. Transfer the chicken to a clean plate and let it cool for a few minutes. When the chicken is cool enough to handle, slice it on an angle across the grain into strips.

About 5 minutes before serving, use a serrated knife to slice the avocado from top to bottom on both sides, allowing the blade to just touch the pit. Set the knife aside and gently twist and pull the avocado halves apart. Remove the pit and gently spoon the avocado out of its skin. Slice it into ¼-inch pieces and drizzle it lightly with lemon juice, coating all surfaces. Set the avocado aside.

To assemble the salad, arrange a bed of romaine and Bibb lettuce on a serving platter or divide the romaine and Bibb lettuces equally among individual plates. Top the lettuce with the chicken, mushrooms, avocado, tomatoes, bacon, and blue cheese. Drizzle the dressing over the salad and season it with salt and pepper to taste.

*Time for Brunch: Make the dressing up to 3 days in advance and store it, covered, in the refrigerator. Stir it well before using it. Allow at least 2 hours and up to 24 hours for marinating the chicken. The salad is best made with chicken warm from the grill, but if you are pressed for time, grill it up to 2 days in advance. Assemble the salad up to 1 hour before you plan to serve it, but don't add the dressing until immediately before serving.*

# grilled wild salmon salad with asparagus and dijon dill dressing

*makes 3 to 4 servings*

*Everybody seems to love salmon, but there's a big difference between the flavor of wild salmon and the more common farm-raised variety. That's because wild salmon store more fat, in order to have the strength to make their long journey upstream to spawn, and this higher fat content makes for absolutely divine eating. It's also good for you, because of the abundance of omega-3 fatty acids in the fat. Yes, the salad will be delicious with farm-raised salmon, but you owe it to yourself to try the wild; it's increasingly available in supermarkets and seafood stores. Because you serve this salad cold, it's a great do-ahead.*

DIJON DILL DRESSING
¼ cup extra-virgin olive oil
Juice of 1 lemon (about
   2 tablespoons)
2 teaspoons Dijon mustard
2 tablespoons fresh chopped dill
Pinch of kosher salt
Pinch of freshly ground black
   pepper

SALMON SALAD
1 pound fresh boneless wild salmon
   fillet

3 tablespoons extra-virgin olive oil
Kosher salt to taste
Freshly ground black pepper to
   taste
4 large asparagus spears, trimmed
   and peeled to remove any bumps
1 large stalk celery, cut diagonally
   into large chunks (about 1 cup)
1 head Bibb lettuce, leaves
   separated, trimmed, washed, and
   dried
Fresh dill sprigs, for garnish
Lemon wedges, for garnish

***To prepare the dressing:*** Whisk the extra-virgin olive oil with the lemon juice, Dijon mustard, and dill in a small glass or stainless steel bowl and season the dressing with salt and pepper to taste. Whisk it until it is well blended.

If you are not serving the salad immediately, cover and refrigerate the dressing.

When you are ready to cook, prepare a charcoal fire or preheat a gas grill to medium-high. Brush the salmon fillets with 2 tablespoons of olive oil and sprinkle both sides with salt and pepper. Brush the asparagus with 1 tablespoon of olive oil and season it with salt and pepper.

Place the salmon fillets on the grill and grill them for 4 to 5 minutes per side. Transfer them to a clean platter, cover them, and refrigerate them for at least 1 hour.

Place the asparagus on the grill and grill it for 2 to 3 minutes, turning it once with tongs. Remove the asparagus from the grill and set it aside to cool. When it is cool enough to handle, cut the spears on a diagonal into 1-inch pieces. If you are not serving the salad immediately, cover and refrigerate the asparagus.

When you are ready to assemble the salad, remove the salmon from the refrigerator, break it into small pieces, and place them into a large bowl. Add the asparagus and celery, pour the dressing over the salad, and toss it gently to coat all the ingredients.

Line a serving platter or individual plates with Bibb lettuce leaves and spoon the salad onto the platter or distribute it among the plates. Garnish the salad with fresh dill sprigs and lemon wedges.

*Time for Brunch: Make the dressing up to 3 days in advance and refrigerate it, covered. Stir it well before using it. You can grill the salmon and asparagus up to 2 days in advance and refrigerate them, covered. Assemble the salad and toss it with the dressing about 30 minutes before serving.*

# sesame noodles

*makes 10 to 12 servings*

*This salad is both beautiful to look at and delightful to eat. It's colorful and intensely flavored, thanks to the combination of ginger and lime. It's the perfect something-a-little-different for your buffet table.*

### SESAME NOODLE SALAD

1 tablespoon kosher salt

1 pound soba noodles

2 cups sugar snap peas, trimmed

1 medium carrot, cut into julienne
    strips (about 1 cup)

½ medium yellow bell pepper,
    seeded and cut into julienne
    strips (about 1 cup)

½ cup bottled roasted red peppers,
    drained and cut into julienne
    strips

3 scallions, trimmed and diced,
    plus 6 more, trimmed, for
    garnish

2 tablespoons sesame seeds

6 lime wedges, for garnish

### LIME GINGER SESAME DRESSING

¾ cup sesame oil

¼ cup rice vinegar

½ cup soy sauce

1 tablespoon fresh lime juice (juice
    of ½ to ¾ lime)

1 large clove garlic, minced

1 tablespoon minced fresh ginger

1 teaspoon freshly ground black
    pepper

> *TIP: Soba noodles are Japanese noodles made from a mixture of buckwheat and wheat flours. They're about the same thickness as spaghetti, but they have a wonderful, almost nutty flavor all their own. If you can't find soba noodles, spaghettini will make a respectable facsimile.*

*To start the noodles:* Fill a large saucepan halfway with water, add 1 tablespoon salt, and bring it to a boil over high heat. Add the soba noodles and cook them for 10 minutes or until they are al dente. Drain them into a colander and rinse them with cold water to stop the cooking process. Pour them into a large stainless steel mixing bowl and set them aside.

*Meanwhile, to prepare the dressing:* Whisk the sesame oil, rice vinegar, soy sauce, lime juice, garlic, ginger, and pepper in a small glass or stainless steel bowl until they are combined. Pour half of the dressing over the noodles. Toss the noodles gently with a rubber spatula until they are well coated and let them stand for 15 minutes.

Add the sugar snap peas, carrots, yellow bell peppers, roasted peppers, and scallions to the noodles. Add the remaining dressing and toss the mixture gently with a rubber spatula until all the vegetables are well coated.

Heat a small sauté or frying pan over high heat. Add the sesame seeds and toast them, tossing them frequently, until they are golden brown. Remove the pan from the heat and transfer the toasted seeds to a small bowl to cool. Be careful not to let the seeds brown too much or burn, or they will be bitter and impart a burned flavor to the salad. If your sesame seeds burn, discard them and toast a new batch.

When you are ready to serve, transfer the salad to a serving bowl or platter and sprinkle it with the toasted sesame seeds. Garnish it with fresh scallions and lime wedges.

*Time for Brunch: Make this salad up to 1 day in advance and refrigerate it, covered. Store any leftovers, covered, in the refrigerator for up to 3 days.*

# wheat berry salad

*makes 8 to 10 servings*

*This is a refreshing salad for a summer day. For the uninitiated, wheat berries are unprocessed wheat kernels. They have a slightly nutty flavor that is a lovely complement for the crunchy vegetables and sweet-tart honey dressing in this salad. This dish does require you to organize your prep in advance, as you have to soak the wheat berries overnight to soften them. After soaking, they'll expand to about twice their size. Serve our Wheat Berry Salad with sandwiches, grilled meat or poultry, or other salads. Its texture and flavor make it different and delightful.*

### WHEAT BERRY SALAD

12 cups cold water

2 cups hard wheat berries

4 ripe large plum tomatoes, seeded
   and cut into ¼-inch chunks
   (about 2 cups)

3 medium cucumbers, peeled,
   seeded, and cut into ¼ inch
   chunks (about 2 heaping cups)

1 (10-ounce) package frozen
   peas

¼ pound snow peas or sugar snap
   peas, trimmed

1 tablespoon chopped fresh mint
   (about 1 ounce)

1 cup chopped fresh parsley

3 teaspoons kosher salt

1 teaspoon freshly ground black
   pepper

### HONEY-LEMON DRESSING

Juice of 3 lemons (about
   6 tablespoons)

1½ cups canola oil

2 teaspoons honey

> *TIP: "Hard" wheat berries are called that after the kind of wheat they come from, a winter variety.*

***To prepare the wheat berries:*** Pour 6 cups of water into a medium saucepan, add the wheat berries, and bring them to a boil over high heat. Remove the pan from the heat and cover it. Soak the wheat berries in the pan overnight.

The next day, drain the wheat berries into a fine-mesh sieve and discard the soaking water. You should have about 4 cups of wheat berries.

Return the soaked, drained wheat berries to the saucepan. Add the remaining 6 cups of water and bring it to a boil. Boil the wheat berries for 10 to 12 minutes. Reduce the heat to a simmer and simmer them, stirring them occasionally, for 1 hour or until they have absorbed most of the water. Drain any excess water and set the wheat berries aside to cool. Then pour them into a medium mixing bowl. You should have about 5 cups of wheat berries.

*To prepare the dressing:* Two hours before serving, whisk the lemon juice, canola oil, and honey in a small glass or stainless steel bowl until the honey is dissolved.

Add the tomatoes and cucumbers to the wheat berries and toss them lightly.

Bring a small saucepan of water to a boil and prepare a bowl of ice water. Add the peas to the boiling water and boil them for 20 seconds or until they turn a brilliant green. Add the snow peas and boil them for 20 seconds. Using a slotted spoon, transfer the peas and snow peas to the ice water and immerse them for 30 seconds. Strain them through a fine-mesh sieve and add them to the wheat berry salad. Add the mint, parsley, salt, and pepper and toss the salad well to incorporate the ingredients.

Pour the dressing over the salad and toss it to coat all the berries and vegetables. Cover the salad and refrigerate it until you are ready to serve.

*Time for Brunch: Allow time to soak the wheat berries overnight so they soften. The salad and dressing are best made about 2 hours before serving. If you are pressed for time, you can make this dish up to 6 hours in advance and store it, covered, in the refrigerator.*

# tomato, basil, and mozzarella platter

*makes 10 to 12 servings*

This is our version of a Caprese salad. Our dressing, laced with pungent capers and olives, gives fine tomatoes and cheese a unique twist. Fresh mozzarella makes all the difference here because of its firm but delicate texture and subtle flavor, which blends perfectly with the tomato and basil. Likewise, a good aged balsamic vinegar imparts a mellow richness without the biting acidity of other vinegars. If you like it hot, the optional crushed red pepper flakes will give the platter a little more oomph.

### GOLDEN PEAR CAPRESE DRESSING

½ cup extra-virgin olive oil

¼ cup high-quality aged balsamic vinegar

¼ cup bottled roasted red peppers, drained

¼ cup finely chopped, drained capers

¼ cup finely chopped pitted kalamata olives

### TOMATO MOZZARELLA SALAD

3 ripe large beefsteak tomatoes or farm tomatoes in season, washed, cored, and sliced into ½-inch rounds

12 medium-large basil leaves, washed and patted dry

1 (16- to 20-ounce) ball fresh mozzarella, cut into ¼-inch rounds

Kosher salt to taste

Freshly ground black pepper to taste

1 teaspoon crushed hot red pepper flakes, optional

*TIP: Balsamic vinegar originated in Modena, Italy. Look for a bottle made there and labeled tradizionale, which means it has been produced in accordance with the traditional rules. Balsamic vinegar should be aged for at least four years; the longer the aging, the richer and mellower the product and the higher the price.*

***To prepare the dressing:*** Whisk the olive oil, vinegar, roasted peppers, capers, and olives in a small glass or stainless steel bowl. Set it aside.

***To prepare the salad:*** Arrange the tomato slices on a large serving platter. Top them with the basil leaves and finish with the mozzarella slices, letting the basil leaves peek out from under the cheese.

Just before serving, whisk the dressing once again and spoon it over the tomato, basil, and mozzarella. Sprinkle the salad with salt, pepper, and hot pepper flakes.

***Time for Brunch:*** *Make the dressing up to 3 days in advance and refrigerate it, covered. Make the salad up to 2 hours in advance and refrigerate it, covered, but don't add the dressing until just before you serve it.*

# country cole slaw

*makes 8 to 10 servings*

*This colorful, creamy cole slaw is an ideal accompaniment for the platter of assorted sandwiches on your brunch tray or for burgers and hot dogs at your backyard barbecue. If you're watching calories, you can use low-fat or no-fat mayonnaise or sour cream with no sacrifice of flavor.*

1 small red cabbage, trimmed, cored, and thinly sliced (about 4 cups)

1 medium green cabbage, trimmed, cored, and thinly sliced (about 8 cups)

2 carrots, grated (about 1 cup)

2 tablespoons chopped fresh parsley

½ cup apple cider vinegar

3 tablespoons granulated sugar

1 cup mayonnaise, preferably Hellmann's

1 cup sour cream

1 teaspoon Worcestershire sauce

Juice of 1 lemon (about 2 tablespoons)

2 teaspoons kosher salt

1 teaspoon freshly ground black pepper

Place the red and green cabbages, carrots, and parsley into a large mixing bowl.

Whisk the cider vinegar and sugar in a separate glass or stainless steel bowl until the sugar is dissolved. Add the mayonnaise, sour cream, Worcestershire sauce, lemon juice, salt, and pepper. Mix it well.

Add the mayonnaise mixture to the cabbage mixture and mix them until all the vegetables are well coated. Cover the slaw and refrigerate it for at least 2 hours before serving.

*Time for Brunch: Make this cole slaw up to 1 day in advance and refrigerate it, covered. If you are preparing it at the last minute, allow at least 2 hours for the slaw to chill, so that the flavors can mingle.*

◄ This is where it all began.

▼ Fresh Baked Muffins and Scones

◄ The perfect omelet

➤ Oh, So Good Oatmeal

▼ Organic Yogurt, Berries, and
Maple Granola

▲ Our Famous Texas Turkey Chili

▲ Grilled Chicken and Jack Cheese Panini

◄ Which way did he go?

MONTAUK
POINT 30M
SAGAPONACK 7M
→

GOOD GROUND 7M
SHINNECOCK
HILLS 3M
EASTPORT 21M
←

▼ Lunch break

▲ Garden Vegetable Lasagna

▲ Cookie, anyone?

▲ Our Amazing Walnut Brownies

▲ Lemon Loaf Cake

▲ Follow me to the Golden Pear.

# roast turkey, brie with herbs, and honey mustard on french bread

· · · · · · · · · · · · · · · · · · · · · · · · · · · · · ·

*makes 8 (6-inch) sandwiches*

*In our first few years in business, in the late 1980s, the composer Marvin Hamlisch came in often, and he always ordered this sandwich. Not long ago he told me this story: "For years I had come to the Golden Pear Cafe and always had the most wonderful turkey sandwich—I think the best I had ever tasted in my whole life. When I proposed to my wife I said, 'To prove to you that you can trust me and that my opinions are pretty valid, I am telling you right now I am going to get you the best turkey sandwich that you've ever tasted.' We drove out to Southampton, and I picked up two turkey sandwiches from the Golden Pear. My wife-to-be tasted one and she said, 'You know, when it comes to food, I think I can trust you.'" I must agree: Young and old alike adore this sandwich. You can roast your own turkey breast—it's easy, the flavor is incomparable, and you'll have leftovers for more sandwiches or for salad. If you're pressed for time, however, store-bought sliced turkey breast is a tasty alternative.*

1 (6- to 8-pound) bone-in fresh turkey breast, or 2 pounds high-quality sliced turkey breast from the deli

1 tablespoon fresh rosemary leaves, optional, for roasting turkey

1 teaspoon kosher salt, optional, for roasting turkey

¼ teaspoon freshly ground black pepper, optional, for roasting turkey

2 (8-ounce) wedges Brie with herbs, ripened

2 (24-inch) fresh French breads

½ cup honey mustard, preferably Honeycup brand

2 medium vine-ripened tomatoes, each cut into 4 (½-inch) slices

8 large leaves green leaf lettuce, trimmed, washed, and dried

2 medium vine-ripened tomatoes, cut into wedges, for garnish

Fresh herb sprigs such as parsley, rosemary, or thyme, for garnish

· · · · · · · · · · · · · · · · · · · · · · · · · · · · · · · · · · · · · · ·

If you are roasting your own turkey breast, preheat the oven to 375 degrees F. Place the turkey breast in a roasting pan, sprinkle it with rosemary leaves, and season it with salt and pepper. Roast the turkey for 1½ to 2 hours or until an instant-read thermometer inserted into the thickest part of the breast reads 160 degrees F. Remove it from the oven and set it aside for 15 minutes. Remove it from the pan, cover it, and refrigerate it for at least 4 hours. Then, using a sharp carving knife, slice about 2 pounds of turkey off the bone and set it aside on a plate. (If you don't have a scale, slice the pieces as thinly as you can — 16 to 32 pieces should be enough for 8 large sandwiches, depending on the thickness of the slices.)

About 10 minutes before you are ready to make the sandwiches, preheat the oven to 250 degrees F. and remove the Brie from the refrigerator to bring it to room temperature. Place the French breads, whole, into the oven for 10 minutes to make them crispy and warm. Remove the bread from the oven and let it stand for about 2 minutes.

Cut each loaf crosswise into 4 equal pieces, cutting on an angle. Then cut each piece in half lengthwise to open it. Arrange the slices face up on a work surface and spread ½ tablespoon of honey mustard on each. Place equal portions of turkey on each of the 8 bottom slices of the bread.

Cut the Brie wedges into 16 (¼-inch) slices. Place 2 slices of Brie and 2 slices of tomato on top of each mound of turkey. Top each with a leaf of lettuce and cover each with the top half of the French bread to complete the sandwiches.

Insert a toothpick on either side of each sandwich. Slice each in half and transfer them to individual plates or a large serving platter. Garnish them with tomato wedges and fresh herbs.

*Time for Brunch:* *If you are roasting your own turkey breast, you can do it up to 2 days in advance; allow at least 4 hours for it to chill before you slice it. The leftover turkey will keep, covered, in the refrigerator for 4 days. We like this sandwich best when it's made with French bread that has been warmed in the oven—and if you heat the bread, you really should dig in and eat it immediately. If you are pressed for time, you can make the sandwich on room-temperature bread a few hours in advance, wrap it, whole, in plastic, and refrigerate it until you are ready to serve. At serving time, unwrap it and cut it up.*

# black forest ham and farmhouse cheddar on sourdough bread

*makes 4 sandwiches or 12 mini sandwiches*

*This sandwich is a taste of the Old World: German-style ham, English farmhouse Cheddar, and spicy French Dijon mustard on a traditional sourdough bread. Put it all together and you'll feel like you've been transported across the Atlantic. We use an entire sourdough bread to make the sandwich and then slice it into big wedges or mini sandwiches for a buffet. Inside, we pile it high with Black Forest ham, a delicacy that originated in the Black Forest of Germany. There, it's made from the choicest pork, which is hand-rubbed in salt or brine and then air-dried and smoked over Black Forest timbers. We use a high-quality American version; it's worth searching around a bit to find one. We like to serve this sandwich with our Country Cole Slaw (page 80).*

1 whole Sourdough Bread (see page 166), or high-quality store-bought sourdough bread

2 to 4 tablespoons Dijon mustard, or to taste

1 pound thinly sliced Black Forest ham

8 to 10 ounces farmhouse Cheddar, sliced by hand

4 large leaves green leaf lettuce, trimmed, washed, and dried, optional

2 medium vine-ripened tomatoes, sliced, optional

½ teaspoon kosher salt

⅛ teaspoon freshly ground black pepper

> *TIP: With Dijon mustard, less is more. It's strong and spicy, and too much can overpower the other flavors of whatever you're cooking.*

Slice the bread in half to make 2 large rounds. Place the 2 halves on a work surface and spread both with Dijon mustard. Place the ham on the bottom half and top it with the Cheddar. If you wish, top the Cheddar with lettuce and tomato. Sprinkle it with salt and pepper and cover it with the top half of the loaf.

Cut the sandwich into quarters and serve them on individual plates or secure it with toothpicks and cut it into as many as 12 pieces for a buffet platter.

*Time for Brunch: Make this sandwich a few hours in advance, wrap it, whole, in plastic, and refrigerate it until you are ready to serve. At serving time, unwrap it and cut it up.*

# grilled flank steak with roasted tomatoes on sourdough bread

. . . . . . . . . . . . . . . . . . . . . . . . . . . . . . . . . .

*makes 6 to 8 servings*

*This mouthwatering sandwich is perfect to serve on the brunch buffet table, but it also makes a great appetizer if you cut the sandwiches into smaller pieces. Roasting plum tomatoes gives them a wonderfully rich flavor that is a perfect counterpoint to the steak.*

FLANK STEAK

2 cups Cabernet Sauvignon

2 cups canned beef broth

½ cup red wine vinegar

2 small bay leaves

1 teaspoon black peppercorns

¼ cup canola oil

1 (2-pound) flank steak

ROASTED TOMATOES

2 to 3 tablespoons olive oil

12 to 14 ripe medium plum tomatoes (about 3 pounds)

Kosher salt to taste

Freshly ground black pepper to taste

1 Sourdough Bread (see page 166), or high-quality store-bought sourdough bread, cut into 18 (½-inch) slices

> *TIP: Grill the meat until it is nicely seared on the outside and rare to medium on the inside. When flank steak is cooked past medium, it becomes tough.*

*To prepare the flank steak marinade:* Bring the wine, beef broth, wine vinegar, bay leaves, and peppercorns to a boil in a small saucepan set over high heat. Immediately remove it from the heat and allow the mixture to cool. Whisk in the canola oil.

. . . . . . . . . . . . . . . . . . . . . . . . . . . . . . . . . . . . . . . . . . .

Place the flank steak into a shallow glass or stainless steel baking dish, pour the cooled marinade over it, and turn the steak to coat it. Cover the dish and refrigerate the steak for 12 hours; then turn it again, cover it, and refrigerate it for 12 hours longer. Repeat the process twice if time allows.

*To prepare the roasted tomatoes:* Preheat the oven to 500 degrees F. Grease a baking sheet with olive oil. Cut the tomatoes in half lengthwise and remove the seeds. Place the tomatoes, cut side down, on the prepared baking sheet. Sprinkle them with salt and pepper. Place the baking sheet on the center rack of the oven and reduce the temperature to 350 degrees F. Roast the tomatoes for 25 minutes. Remove them from the oven and allow them to cool. If you are not proceeding with the rest of the recipe immediately, transfer them to a storage container, cover it, and refrigerate them for up to 2 days.

Ten minutes before you plan to grill the steak, remove it from the refrigerator. Prepare a charcoal fire or preheat a gas grill to high. Place the steak on the grill and discard any remaining marinade. Grill the steak for 3 to 4 minutes per side, turning it with tongs. Remove the steak from the grill, place it on a clean platter, and let it rest for a few minutes. Slice the meat very thinly, on a slight angle, cutting against the grain.

Arrange half the bread in a single layer on a work surface. Divide the sliced steak evenly among the slices, top each with about 1 tablespoon of roasted tomatoes, and cover each with a slice of bread. Garnish the sandwiches with fresh parsley, basil, or rosemary sprigs and serve them immediately.

*Time for Brunch: You can roast the tomatoes 2 days in advance and store them, covered, in the refrigerator. For maximum flavor, marinate the steak, covered, in the refrigerator, for 2 days. (If you are pressed for time, 24 hours will do.) Don't grill the steak until just before you plan to serve it, or it will become tough.*

# grilled chicken, jack cheese, caramelized onion, and chipotle dressing panini

*makes 4 whole sandwiches*

*Here's an Old World meets New World twist on the traditional Italian panini sandwich. The bread is Italian, but the fillings—chicken and caramelized onions with Monterey Jack cheese and a chipotle dressing that you make yourself—are very American. To make a panini, you'll need a panini grill press, a small investment that will give any sandwich you make a whole new life. Your bread will be crispy and warm, the cheese will melt and run out the sides a bit, and the whole thing will be positively scrumptious. If you don't have a panini press, assemble the sandwich and cook it like a grilled cheese in an oiled frying pan weighted down with a spatula or a small plate. It won't be exactly like a panini, but it will still taste great. Do use the best sourdough ciabatta bread you can find.*

### GRILLED CHICKEN AND JACK CHEESE PANINI

5 tablespoons canola oil

Juice of ½ lemon (about 1 tablespoon)

½ teaspoon kosher salt

¼ teaspoon freshly ground black pepper

1 pound skinless, boneless chicken breast cutlets, trimmed

1 large sweet onion such as Vidalia, cut into ¼-inch slices

4 (6-inch) high-quality ciabatta breads

6 ounces sliced Monterey Jack cheese

Nonstick vegetable oil spray

### CHIPOTLE DRESSING

½ cup mayonnaise, preferably Hellmann's

¼ cup sour cream

2 tablespoons canned chipotles in adobo sauce, chopped

2 tablespoons canned green chilies, drained and minced

2 tablespoons canned black beans, rinsed, drained, and minced

Juice of ½ lime (about 1 teaspoon)

¼ teaspoon Worcestershire sauce

*TIP: Chipotles are smoked jalapeño chili peppers beloved by Mexican and, increasingly, American cooks. Their spicy-hot, smoky flavor adds a new dimension to many dishes.*

*To prepare the chicken:* Make a marinade by whisking 2 tablespoons of canola oil and the lemon juice, salt, and pepper in a shallow glass or stainless steel baking dish. Place the chicken into the dish in a single layer and turn it with tongs to coat it thoroughly. Cover it and refrigerate it for at least 30 minutes.

*Meanwhile, to caramelize the onions:* Heat the remaining 3 tablespoons of canola oil in a small sauté pan set over medium heat. Add the onions and sauté them, stirring them and shaking the pan frequently, for about 10 minutes or until they are very soft and browned. Transfer the onions to a bowl.

*To prepare the dressing:* Whisk the mayonnaise and sour cream in a small glass or stainless steel bowl until they are well blended. Add the chipotles, green chilies, black beans, lime juice, and Worcestershire sauce and whisk the mixture for 30 seconds or until all the ingredients are well blended. Cover the dressing and refrigerate it until you are ready to assemble the sandwich.

Ten minutes before you plan to grill the chicken, remove it from the refrigerator. Prepare a charcoal fire or preheat a gas grill to high. Place the chicken on the grill in a single layer and discard any remaining marinade. Grill the chicken for 3 to 4 minutes per side or until it is no longer pink, the juices run clear, and an instant-read thermometer inserted into the thickest part of the cutlet reads 160 degrees F. Transfer the chicken to a clean plate and let it cool for a few minutes. When the chicken is cool enough to handle, slice it on an angle across the grain into ½-inch strips and set it aside.

Preheat the panini grill to 375 degrees F. (It will take about 10 minutes.) Preheat the oven to 185 degrees F.

Slice open the ciabatta breads and arrange them face up on a work surface. Spread about 1 tablespoon of chipotle dressing on each slice. (You will have leftover dressing.) Place equal portions of chicken on the 4 bottom slices of ciabatta. Top each with equal portions of caramelized onion and Monterey Jack cheese. Place the top pieces of the bread on top.

Spray the panini grill with nonstick vegetable oil spray. Place 2 sandwiches into it (most will accommodate 2 at a time), close the lid, and press it down to flatten the sandwiches to half their original height. Leave the lid closed for 1 minute and then test to see if the bread has been toasted and marked by the grill. If not, close it for 1 minute longer. Remove the paninis from the press, transfer them to a roasting pan, cover it with aluminum foil, and place the pan into the oven. Repeat the process with the 2 remaining sandwiches.

To serve, cut the sandwiches in half on a diagonal and place them on individual plates or insert 4 toothpicks into each sandwich, cut the sandwiches into quarters, and arrange them on a large serving platter for your buffet.

*Time for Brunch: Make these sandwiches up to 1 hour in advance; place them into a roasting pan, cover it with aluminum foil, and hold them in a 185-degree oven. The recipe for Chipotle Dressing above makes about 2 cups. Refrigerate leftover dressing, covered, for up to 5 days.*

# hummus and grated veggies in whole wheat pita

*makes 4 sandwiches (8 pita pockets) or 8 mini sandwiches (16 pita pockets)*

*What sets our hummus apart from the rest is a touch of honey—it's delicious. This classic Middle Eastern treat is perfect for the vegetarians on your guest list and tasty enough for all the others. The hummus is a fast, easy, do-ahead item and the sandwich assembly is a snap. If you really want to be extra, extra good, use organic veggies for this healthy sandwich. We like to serve this with another vegetarian favorite, our Wheat Berry Salad (page 76).*

### HUMMUS

¾ cup sesame tahini, stirred before measuring

1 (15.5-ounce) can garbanzo beans (chickpeas), rinsed and drained (about 2 cups)

1 medium clove garlic, cut into large pieces

Juice of 2 lemons (about ¼ cup)

½ cup water, preferably filtered

1 teaspoon honey

1 teaspoon kosher salt

### PITA SANDWICHES

4 (7-inch) whole-wheat pita breads or 8 whole-wheat mini pitas

2 tablespoons bottled Italian dressing, optional

2 carrots, grated (about 1 cup)

1 small zucchini, grated (about 1 cup)

12 thin slices cucumber

2 medium vine-ripened tomatoes, sliced

2 cups alfalfa sprouts

> TIP: *Sesame tahini is a paste made of sesame seeds with a wonderfully rich, nutty flavor. It's available in many supermarkets and Middle Eastern markets. The sesame oil has a tendency to separate from the solids, so stir it well each time you use it.*

*To prepare the hummus:* Before measuring out the tahini, stir it to blend any oil that has risen to the top back into the paste. Spoon ¾ cup of tahini into a food processor fitted with a metal blade, add the garbanzo beans and garlic, and process the mixture at high speed for 3 to 4 minutes or until it forms a coarse paste. While the food processor is running, add the lemon juice, water, honey, and salt. Process the hummus for 2 minutes longer or until it is smooth. Using a spatula, scoop the hummus into an airtight container. Refrigerate it until you are ready to assemble the sandwiches.

*To assemble the sandwiches:* Slice the pita breads in half crosswise to make 2 pockets. Gently open each pocket. If you are using 7-inch pitas, spread about 2 tablespoons of hummus into each pocket. If you are using mini pitas, spread 1 tablespoon into each pocket. If you wish, pour the Italian dressing into a small bowl, add the grated carrots and zucchini, and toss the vegetables to coat them. Place equal portions of grated carrots and zucchini into each pocket and follow with equal portions of cucumber and tomatoes. Add equal portions of sprouts to complete the sandwiches.

To serve, place the stuffed pockets on individual plates or on a large serving platter for a buffet.

*Time for Brunch: You can make the hummus up to 3 days in advance and refrigerate it, covered. If you don't use the Italian dressing on the grated veggies, you can assemble the sandwiches up to 2 hours in advance and store them, covered, in the refrigerator. If you use the dressing, assemble the sandwiches and serve them immediately. Freeze any leftover hummus, tightly covered, for up to 2 months.*

# southwestern grilled chicken wrap

*makes 4 whole wraps or 8 half wraps
or 16 to 32 small pieces*

*Our number-one selling wrap year after year. It's a tasty combination of fresh grilled chicken, Monterey Jack cheese, and our own chunky guacamole and spicy salsa. You can serve these wraps as a main course on your brunch buffet table or cut them up into smaller pieces and serve them at a party as an appetizer. Mix up a batch of margaritas and enjoy them with these delectable wraps.*

½ cup canola oil

Juice of 2 limes (about ¼ cup)

1 teaspoon kosher salt

¼ teaspoon freshly ground black pepper

1¼ pounds skinless, boneless chicken breast cutlets, trimmed

4 (12-inch) flour tortillas

¾ cup Guacamole (see page 161), or store-bought guacamole

½ cup Spicy Tomato Salsa (see page 160), or salsa from the supermarket's refrigerated section

8 (1-ounce) slices Monterey Jack cheese

2 medium vine-ripened tomatoes, each cut into 4 (½-inch) slices

¼ head green leaf lettuce, cut into 4 large pieces, trimmed, washed, and dried

2 medium vine-ripened tomatoes, cut into wedges, for garnish

3 limes, cut into wedges, for garnish

Fresh cilantro sprigs, for garnish

*TIP: Whenever you marinate poultry, meat, or fish, it's safest to do so in the refrigerator to prevent the growth of any bacteria. When it's time to cook, take the marinated food out of the fridge and let it stand for ten minutes before you put it on the grill or into the oven. This will take the chill off and make for even cooking.*

*To prepare the chicken:* Make a marinade by whisking the canola oil, lime juice, salt, and pepper in a shallow glass or stainless steel baking dish. Place the chicken into the dish in a single layer and turn it with tongs to coat it thoroughly. Cover it and refrigerate it for at least 30 minutes.

Ten minutes before you plan to cook the chicken, remove it from the refrigerator. Prepare a charcoal fire or preheat a gas grill to high. Place the chicken on the grill in a single layer and discard any remaining marinade. Grill the chicken for 4 minutes per side or until it is no longer pink, the juices run clear, and an instant-read thermometer inserted into the thickest part of the breast reads 160 degrees F. Transfer the chicken to a clean plate and let it cool for a few minutes. When the chicken is cool enough to handle, slice it on an angle across the grain into ¼-inch strips.

Place the tortillas on a clean work surface. Spoon one-fourth of the guacamole into the center of each tortilla and spread it to cover a 6 × 2-inch strip. Top each with one-fourth of the chicken. Spoon one-fourth of the salsa over the chicken. Place 2 slices of Monterey Jack cheese and 2 slices of tomato on top of each. Top each with an equal portion of lettuce.

*To wrap the tortilla:* Fold the left and right edges in toward the center. Fold the edge closest to you toward the center; then roll the entire wrap away from you to seal it, with the seam on the bottom. Insert a toothpick into each side to hold it together. The more pieces you want to cut, the more toothpicks you will need to ensure that the wraps don't fall open. You can insert up to 6 toothpicks into each wrap to make up to 8 pieces per wrap.

With a sharp serrated knife, slice each wrap in half on a diagonal. To serve 4, place 2 halves on each individual plate. To serve more: Cut the halves in half for 8 pieces; in quarters for 16 pieces; or in as many pieces as you wish (you can safely get 8 rounds out of a wrap if you secure it with 6 toothpicks). Garnish the wraps with tomato wedges, lime wedges, and fresh cilantro sprigs.

*Time for Brunch: Make this tasty wrap the night before you plan to serve it, wrap it in plastic, whole, and refrigerate it overnight. Unwrap it and cut it up just before serving.*

# grilled vegetables and fresh mozzarella wrap

*makes 4 whole wraps or 8 half wraps*

*An ideal brunch item for the vegetarians at your table. Fresh mozzarella is a must here. Find an Italian market or a good deli that makes it on the premises, and go early to be sure they aren't sold out before you get there—good fresh mozzarella has a tendency to disappear fast. You can prep the veggies ahead, but roll these wraps right before you serve them; the vinaigrette will make them soggy if you let them sit for too long. Nor do we recommend cutting this wrap into small pieces, as the vegetables will fall out. Go ahead and enjoy a big hunk—besides being delicious, all those veggies are good for you.*

1 medium zucchini, cut lengthwise into ¼-inch strips

1 medium yellow squash, cut lengthwise into ¼-inch strips

1 medium Japanese eggplant, cut lengthwise into ¼-inch strips

1 medium carrot, cut lengthwise into ¼-inch strips

1 red bell pepper, seeded and cut into quarters

1 yellow bell pepper, seeded and cut into quarters

½ cup olive oil

1 teaspoon kosher salt

¼ teaspoon freshly ground black pepper

½ cup Balsamic Vinaigrette (see page 158)

1 pound fresh mozzarella

20 large fresh basil leaves

4 (12-inch) plain or sun-dried-tomato flour tortillas

4 ripe medium plum or vine-ripened tomatoes, cut into wedges, for garnish

To grill the vegetables, prepare a charcoal fire or preheat a gas grill to high. Place the zucchini, yellow squash, eggplant, carrot, and red and yellow peppers into a large bowl. Drizzle the olive oil over the vegetables and season them with salt and pepper. Toss to coat thoroughly.

Place the vegetables on the grill in a single layer and grill them for 3 minutes per side or until they are tender and have attractive grill markings.

Transfer them to a plate and let them cool for a few minutes. When the vegetables are cool enough to handle, cut them into 1-inch chunks and place them into a large glass or stainless steel bowl. Pour the balsamic vinaigrette over the vegetables and toss them to coat them. Let them stand for a few minutes.

Meanwhile, slice the mozzarella into 4 pieces and then slice each piece in half to make 8 half-moon-shaped pieces. Wash the basil leaves and pat them dry.

Place the tortillas on a work surface. Spoon one-fourth of the grilled vegetables into the center of each tortilla. Top each with 2 pieces of mozzarella and 3 basil leaves.

To wrap the tortilla, fold the left and right edges in toward the center. Fold the edge closest to you toward the center; then roll the entire wrap away from you to seal it, with the seam on the bottom. Insert a toothpick into each side to hold it together.

With a sharp serrated knife, slice each wrap in half on a diagonal. Transfer the wraps to a serving platter and garnish them with tomato wedges and the remaining fresh basil leaves.

*Time for Brunch: You can prep the veggies ahead of time, but assemble the wraps just prior to serving so they don't become soggy.*

# 5 · main courses

## The Swimsuit Competition

On sum-
mer weekends,
any single guys who hap-
pen to be in the cafe at
around 11:00 A.M. suddenly
have trouble concentrat-
ing on their food, because
they're so busy turning
their heads to check out
the new arrivals. I can't

◄ Savory Chicken Pot Pie

blame them; some of the bikini briefs are, well, brief! Sometimes the singles do more than check each other out, and we've had quite a few matches made in the cafes.

In the kitchen, though, no swimsuits are allowed; there's fast, heavy work to be done, and we can't risk our people getting burned or otherwise injured. They're preparing catering orders at a furious pace, piling up platters of sandwiches in the walk-in refrigerator, and whisking poached salmons and guacamole-and-salsa platters out the side door to waiting cars. Members of the kitchen crew are competing for prep space on the kitchen's tiny tables. I poke my head into the kitchen and ask my two lead guys, "Everything okay?" They assure me that all orders will be done on time. Where would I be without Pablo and Alfredo?

Back in the cafe area, the bathing beauties are blissfully unaware of the frenzy taking place on the other side of the wall. Some of them are obviously enjoying showing off a bit. As the owner, it's my responsibility to make sure the atmosphere at the Golden Pear is always suitable for families and young ones, so occasionally I have to ask someone to put on a coverup. It's a tough job, but someone's got to do it.

# savory chicken pot pie

*makes 1 (9 × 14-inch) pie (10 to 12 servings)*

*In August 1991, forecasters were predicting that Hurricane Bob would reach the Hamptons around noon. That, however, didn't keep people away from breakfast at the Golden Pear. At 11:00 A.M., New York City TV anchorman Chuck Scarborough came into the Southampton cafe with a handheld video camera. He started interviewing people, asking them if they realized that a hurricane was going to hit soon and what they planned to do. Since then we've seen Chuck often; he likes to buy our chicken pot pies as takeout. In addition to a nose for news, he's got a nose for good food! Our version of this All-American classic makes use of both homemade Golden Pear piecrust and store-bought puff pastry for the lattice top. If you don't have time to make the crust from scratch, substitute two store-bought piecrusts.*

### GOLDEN PEAR PIECRUST

2¼ sticks (1⅛ cups) cold unsalted
    butter

3 cups all-purpose flour

½ teaspoon kosher salt

⅓ cup cold water, preferably
    filtered

### CHICKEN FILLING

8 cups Golden Pear Chicken Stock
    (see page 155), or canned
    chicken stock

1¼ cups water, preferably filtered

3 pounds boneless, skinless chicken
    breasts

1 medium onion, cut into ½-inch
    cubes (about 2 cups)

3 to 4 carrots, cut into ½-inch cubes
    (about 2 cups)

3 to 3½ large stalks celery, cut into
    ½-inch cubes (about 1¾ cups)

4 large red potatoes, peeled and cut
    into ½-inch pieces (about 2 cups)

8 ounces frozen peas (about 1½
    cups), rinsed quickly under
    warm water

1½ sticks (¾ cup) unsalted butter

¾ cup all-purpose flour

1 sprig fresh rosemary

¼ cup chopped fresh parsley

1 teaspoon Worcestershire sauce

2 teaspoons kosher salt

¾ teaspoon freshly ground black
    pepper

1 (17.3-ounce) box frozen puff
    pastry sheets, thawed

1 large egg

Fresh parsley sprigs, for garnish

*To prepare the piecrust:* If you are making your piecrust from scratch, combine the butter, flour, and salt in a large bowl. Using an electric mixer set at low speed, mix them for 3 to 5 minutes or until most of the butter is incorporated into the flour. Add the water and mix it in at low speed for 1 minute or until a dough forms. Transfer the dough to a work surface and form it into a ball. Wrap it in plastic wrap, pat it into a disk shape, and let it rest in a cool spot for 30 minutes. If you are using store-bought piecrusts, thaw them.

*To prepare the filling:* Bring the chicken stock and 1 cup of water to a boil in a large stockpot set over high heat. Reduce the heat to medium, carefully place the chicken breasts into the stock, and poach them for 15 to 20 minutes or until they are cooked through and no longer pink and an instant-read thermometer inserted into the thickest part of the breast reads 160 degrees F. Remove them from the heat.

When the dough has rested for 30 minutes, roll it into a 14 × 20-inch rectangle. If you are using store-bought crusts, combine them and roll them into a 14 × 20-inch rectangle. Roll the dough onto your rolling pin and unroll it over a 9 × 14-inch casserole or baking dish, tucking it into the corners with your fingers. The dough should overhang the edge of the dish by about ½ inch. Flute this edge with a fork or your fingers. Prick the bottom of the crust with a fork to prevent air bubbles from forming. Let the crust rest, uncovered, in the refrigerator for 30 minutes or in the freezer for 10 minutes.

With tongs or a slotted spoon, transfer the chicken onto a work surface. Reserve the stock in the stockpot. When the chicken is cool enough to handle, cut it into ½-inch pieces, removing any fat, and place the pieces into a large bowl.

Add the onions, carrots, and celery to the reserved chicken stock and set the stockpot over medium-high heat. Cook the vegetables for 4 to 5 minutes or until they are just slightly tender. With a slotted spoon, transfer the vegetables into the bowl with the chicken. Reserve the stock in the stockpot. Add the potatoes to the stock and cook them over medium-high heat for 4 to 5 minutes or until they are cooked through but slightly firm. With a slotted spoon, transfer the potatoes to the chicken-vegetable mixture. Reserve the stock in the stockpot. Add the peas to the chicken and vegetables.

Preheat the oven to 375 degrees F. Make a roux: Melt the butter in a small saucepan set over low heat. Whisk in the flour and cook the mixture, stirring it constantly, for 2 to 3 minutes or until the flour is thoroughly dissolved and the roux is golden blond in color and will coat the back of a spoon. Be careful not to let it burn. Remove it from the heat and keep it warm.

Remove the piecrust from the refrigerator or freezer and bake it, unfilled, for 15 to 20 minutes or until it is very lightly browned.

Meanwhile, make the sauce by removing the leaves from the rosemary sprig and adding them to the reserved stock. Add the parsley, Worcestershire sauce, salt, and pepper. Add the warm roux, bring the mixture to a boil, and stir it with a wire whisk for 1 minute or until the ingredients are well blended and the sauce is thickened enough to coat the back of a spoon. Pour the sauce over the chicken and vegetables.

Cut the puff pastry into ½-inch strips and set it aside.

Make an egg wash: Using a fork, gently beat the egg lightly with ¼ cup water in a cup or small bowl. Set it aside.

When the crust is baked, remove it from the oven and spoon the warm chicken and vegetable mixture into it, pouring all the sauce over the top. Interweave the puff pastry strips in a lattice pattern on top of the filled crust and press it with your fingertips to attach it to the edges. Use a pastry brush to brush the lattice and edges with the egg wash. Bake the pie for 35 to 40 minutes or until the pastry is golden brown and the filling bubbles. Remove the pie from the oven and let it rest for 10 minutes.

To serve, cut it into squares and place each one into a soup bowl. Garnish each serving with fresh parsley sprigs.

*Time for Brunch: This dish is best made the day you plan to eat it, but if you are pressed for time, you can make it up to 3 days in advance. Refrigerate it, covered, and reheat it, uncovered, in a 350-degree oven for 45 minutes to 1 hour; an instant-read thermometer inserted into the center should read 160 degrees F.*

# southwestern
# chicken casserole

*makes 10 to 12 servings*

*This lively Southwestern casserole is lovely as a main course, but it's also great as an appetizer to accompany margaritas, guacamole, and chips. It's a great do-ahead. Cook the chicken on the grill or sear it in a pan on the stove; either way works. Bake the casserole in a baking dish that can go right from the oven to the table. If you like your Tex-Mex foods on the hot side, add a bit of hot sauce in addition to the spicy salsa. Serve it with your favorite tortilla chips; we like the kind made from organic blue corn.*

¼ cup plus 2 tablespoons olive oil,
  plus ¼ cup, for pan-searing

Juice of 4 limes (about ½ cup)

2½ pounds boneless, skinless
  chicken breast cutlets, trimmed

½ medium onion, cut into ¼-inch
  cubes (about 1 cup)

3 medium cloves garlic, chopped

8 to 10 ripe medium plum tomatoes
  (2 pounds), seeded and diced

1 cup kalamata olives, drained,
  pitted, and sliced

1 jalapeño pepper, seeds and ribs
  removed, finely diced

2 cups Spicy Tomato Salsa (see
  page 160), or tomato salsa from
  the supermarket's refrigerated
  section

1 tablespoon hot pepper sauce such
  as Tabasco, or to taste, optional

1 (15.5-ounce) can black beans,
  rinsed and drained

2 cups grated Cheddar cheese
  (8 ounces)

2 cups grated Monterey Jack
  cheese (8 ounces)

1 cup sour cream

¼ cup plus 1 tablespoon finely
  chopped fresh cilantro

2 teaspoons kosher salt

½ teaspoon freshly ground black
  pepper

1 large bag of your favorite tortilla
  chips

To prepare the chicken, make a marinade by whisking 2 tablespoons of olive oil and ½ cup of fresh lime juice in a shallow glass or stainless steel baking dish. Place the chicken into the dish and turn it with tongs to coat both sides thoroughly. Cover it and refrigerate it for at least 2 hours or up to 24 hours.

Ten minutes before you plan to cook the chicken, remove it from the refrigerator. If you are grilling, prepare a charcoal fire or preheat a gas grill to high. Place the chicken on the grill in a single layer and discard any remaining marinade. Grill the chicken for 3 to 4 minutes per side, turning it frequently. If you are pan-searing, heat ¼ cup of olive oil in a skillet set over medium-high heat until it sizzles and swirl the skillet to coat the surface. Carefully place the chicken into the skillet in a single layer and cook it for about 6 minutes per side. With either method, cook the chicken until it is no longer pink, the juices run clear, and an instant-read thermometer inserted into the thickest part of the breast reads 160 degrees F. Transfer the cooked chicken to a clean plate, cover it, and refrigerate it for 20 to 30 minutes or until it is cool. When the chicken is cool enough to handle, cut it into bite-sized pieces. Set it aside.

Meanwhile, heat ¼ cup of olive oil in a skillet set over medium-high heat. Add the onions and sauté them, stirring them and shaking the pan, for about 7 minutes or until they are softened and golden. Add the garlic, reduce the heat to medium, and cook the mixture for 1 minute. Set aside ½ cup of the plum tomatoes. Add the rest of them to the skillet and cook the mixture for about 2 minutes or until the tomatoes are just barely softened.

Preheat the oven to 375 degrees F. Pour the vegetables into a large baking dish or casserole. Add the chicken, black beans, olives, jalapeño pepper, salsa, and hot sauce, 1½ cups of Cheddar and 1½ cups of Monterey Jack cheese, the sour cream, ¼ cup of cilantro, and the salt and pepper. Stir the mixture to blend all the ingredients well. Top it with the remaining ½ cup of Cheddar and ½ cup of Monterey Jack cheese. Bake the casserole for about 1 hour and 10 minutes or until it is browned and bubbly. Remove it from the oven and let it rest for 10 minutes.

Garnish the casserole with the remaining 1 tablespoon of chopped cilantro and ½ cup of diced tomatoes and serve it with tortilla chips.

*Time for Brunch: Make this casserole up to 3 days in advance and refrigerate it, covered. Reheat it in a 350-degree oven for 45 minutes to 1 hour or until an instant-read thermometer inserted into the center reads 160 degrees F.*

# turkey meatloaf
## makes 2 (9 × 4-inch) loaves (10 to 12 servings)

*This is good old-fashioned comfort food, lightened up with ground turkey in place of beef. Serve it with homemade turkey gravy if you're feeling traditional. (If you don't have time to roast a turkey to make turkey stock for the gravy recipe below, chicken stock will do just fine.) Or liven it up with barbecue sauce for something a little different. Mashed or roasted potatoes will make it a hearty meal.*

TURKEY MEATLOAF
Nonstick vegetable oil spray
3 medium or 1½ large onions,
    coarsely chopped (about 1½ cups)
4 cloves garlic
¼ cup sun-dried tomatoes
3½ pounds lean ground turkey
½ cup grated Parmesan cheese
2 large eggs
¼ cup canned tomato paste
1 cup dry bread crumbs
2 tablespoons chopped fresh parsley
1 tablespoon dried oregano
1 tablespoon kosher salt
1 teaspoon freshly ground black
    pepper

Bottled barbecue sauce,
    optional

TURKEY GRAVY, OPTIONAL
3 cups turkey stock, Golden Pear
    Chicken Stock (see page 155), or
    canned chicken stock
½ stick (¼ cup) unsalted butter
½ medium shallot, minced
    (2 tablespoons)
4 tablespoons all-purpose flour
¼ teaspoon Gravy Master
1 teaspoon fresh rosemary leaves
Kosher salt to taste
Freshly ground black pepper to
    taste

> *TIP: Gravy Master is a very useful seasoning and coloring product made of concentrated spices and caramel coloring. It's been on the market forever (well, actually, since 1935). We use it because it gives our turkey gravy a nice medium-brown color without the labor- and time-intensive step of browning the bones before making the stock.*

Preheat the oven to 375 degrees F. Spray 2 (9 × 4-inch) loaf pans with nonstick vegetable oil spray.

*To prepare the meatloaf:* Combine the onions, garlic, and sun-dried tomatoes in a food processor fitted with a metal blade. Process them until the mixture is smooth and creamy.

Pour the onion puree into a large bowl and add the ground turkey, Parmesan cheese, eggs, tomato paste, bread crumbs, parsley, oregano, salt, and pepper. Mix the ingredients thoroughly. Scrape the mixture into the prepared pans, smooth the tops with a rubber spatula, and bake the meatloaves for about 1 hour or until an instant-read thermometer inserted into the center of a loaf reads 165 degrees F. (For barbecue-style meatloaf, invert the loaves onto a roasting pan, pour the barbecue sauce over the loaves, and spread it to cover them. Bake them for 10 minutes longer.)

*If you are serving homemade turkey gravy:* Prepare it while the meatloaves are baking. Bring the stock to a boil in a small saucepan set over medium-high heat. Reduce the heat to low.

Meanwhile, make a roux: In a separate small saucepan, melt the butter over medium heat. Add the shallots and sauté them, stirring them and shaking the pan, for 1 minute or until they are softened and translucent. Whisk in the flour and cook the mixture, stirring it constantly, for 1 to 2 minutes or until the flour is thoroughly dissolved and the roux is golden blond in color. Be careful not to let it burn.

Slowly pour the stock into the roux and whisk it in thoroughly. Simmer it for 1 minute.

Bring the gravy to a boil; then reduce the heat to low. Add the Gravy Master and whisk the gravy for 30 seconds to blend it in. Add the rosemary, salt, and pepper and simmer the gravy, stirring it occasionally, for 10 minutes. Keep it warm until you are ready to serve.

When you are ready to serve, place the meatloaves on a serving platter. If you have gravy, pour a generous amount over the tops of the loaves. Serve any remaining gravy in a gravy boat.

*Time for Brunch: Make this tasty dish 3 days in advance and refrigerate it, covered. Refrigerate the gravy separately. Reheat the meatloaf in a roasting pan, covered, in a 350-degree oven for 45 minutes to 1 hour or until an instant-read thermometer inserted into the center reads 160 degrees F. Reheat the gravy in a small saucepan set over medium heat until it is heated through.*

main courses  105

# american shepherd's pie

*True enough, the original shepherd's pie was not made with ground turkey, but turkey definitely lightens up this hearty dish, with no sacrifice of flavor—and since the turkey is such a popular bird in the USA, we thought we'd change the name. Bake this pie in a casserole dish that can go from oven to table. You can use convenient frozen corn and peas, but do use fresh leaf spinach; it will make a real difference in the pie's flavor and texture.*

### MASHED POTATO TOPPING
6 russet potatoes (about 4 pounds), peeled and cut into 1-inch cubes (about 12 cups)
3 tablespoons unsalted butter
1½ cups half and half
3 teaspoons kosher salt
1 teaspoon freshly ground black pepper

### SPINACH LAYER
1 tablespoon olive oil
10 ounces triple-washed fresh leaf spinach, trimmed and dried

### GRAVY
¼ stick (2 tablespoons) unsalted butter
3 tablespoons all-purpose flour
1¾ cups canned beef broth

### SHEPHERD'S PIE FILLING
Nonstick vegetable oil spray
2 tablespoons olive oil

2 pounds lean ground turkey
½ large Spanish onion, chopped (about 1½ cups)
2 medium garlic cloves, minced
1 teaspoon dried oregano
1 teaspoon chopped fresh basil
2½ to 3 medium carrots, cut into ½-inch cubes (about 1½ cups)
¼ cup canned beef broth
1 cup canned crushed tomatoes, drained
1 (6-ounce) can tomato paste (¾ cup)
1 pound frozen corn kernels, thawed, or corn kernels shucked from 6 large ears of corn (2½ to 3 cups)
1 pound frozen petite peas (2½ to 3 cups), rinsed quickly under warm water
Kosher salt to taste
Freshly ground pepper to taste

*To prepare the topping:* Place the potatoes into a stockpot with enough water to cover them. Bring them to a boil over high heat and cook them for 10 to 12 minutes or until they are tender and easy to pierce with the tip of a knife. Drain the potatoes and return them to the pot. Add 3 tablespoons of butter and the half and half, salt, and pepper and mash the potatoes with a potato masher until they are creamy. Set them aside and keep them warm.

*To prepare the spinach:* Heat 1 tablespoon of olive oil in a sauté pan set over medium-high heat and swirl the pan to coat the surface. Add the spinach and sauté it, stirring it to coat it with the oil, for about 1 minute or until it just begins to wilt. Remove it from the heat and set it aside.

*To prepare the gravy:* Make a roux: Melt 2 tablespoons of butter in a small saucepan set over low heat. Whisk in the flour and cook the mixture, stirring it constantly, for 2 minutes or until the flour is thoroughly dissolved and the roux is golden blond in color and will coat the back of a spoon. Be careful not to let it burn. Add 1¾ cups of beef broth, whisk it in thoroughly, and bring the gravy to a boil. Reduce the heat to low and simmer the gravy, stirring it occasionally, for 5 minutes. Remove the pan from the heat and set it aside.

*To prepare the filling:* Preheat the oven to 400 degrees F. Spray a 9 × 14 × 2½-inch casserole dish with nonstick vegetable oil spray.

Heat 2 tablespoons of olive oil in a skillet set over medium heat until it sizzles and swirl the skillet to coat the surface. Add the ground turkey and cook it, stirring it and mashing it with a wooden spoon to break up any large clumps, for about 7 minutes or until it is browned. Carefully drain off any fat. Add the onions, garlic, oregano, and basil and sauté the mixture, stirring it and shaking the pan, for about 3 minutes or until the onions are soft and translucent. Add the carrots and ¼ cup of beef broth. Sauté the mixture, stirring, for about 4 minutes. Add the crushed tomatoes and tomato paste and bring the mixture to a simmer. Add the corn and peas and cook the mixture for about 3 minutes or just until they are heated through. (The peas should be green, not golden.)

Add the gravy to the turkey filling, season the mixture with salt and pepper to taste, and stir it well to incorporate all the ingredients. Pour it into the prepared casserole dish. Spoon the spinach evenly over the turkey filling. Spoon the mashed potatoes on top of the spinach and spread them gently to make an even layer. Bake the pie for about 30 minutes or until the potatoes are lightly browned. Serve it hot.

*Time for Brunch: Make this dish up to 3 days in advance. Just before serving, reheat it in a 350-degree oven for 40 to 45 minutes.*

# seared sesame tuna
# with pacific wasabi sauce
· · · · · · · · · · · · · · · · · · · · · · · · · · · · · · · · ·

*makes 12 to 15 servings*

*The only way to make this light, healthy, and very flavorful tuna is with a 12-inch cast-iron skillet. If you don't have one, get one; the investment will be worth it for this dish alone. We use peanut oil for this dish because it holds up under very high heat; however, the high heat renders it bitter, so once you use the oil for this recipe it should be discarded. If you or a guest is allergic to nuts, by all means use canola oil instead. Be careful with the wasabi paste; it's hot stuff!*

**SEARED SESAME TUNA**

4 pounds fresh sushi-grade tuna, cut into 5- or 6-inch × 2-inch loins

½ cup soy sauce

½ cup balsamic vinegar

2 cups sesame seeds

½ cup peanut oil or canola oil

**WASABI SAUCE**

1½ cups mayonnaise, preferably Hellmann's

½ cup sour cream

1 teaspoon Dijon mustard

Juice of ½ lime (about 1 tablespoon)

1 teaspoon kosher salt

½ teaspoon freshly ground black pepper

6 tablespoons authentic wasabi paste

4 limes, cut into wedges, for garnish

***To prepare the tuna:*** Make a marinade by whisking the soy sauce and balsamic vinegar in a glass or stainless steel baking dish. Place the tuna into the dish in a single layer and turn it with tongs to coat all sides. Cover it and refrigerate it for at least 2 hours and up to 24 hours.

Ten minutes before you plan to cook the tuna, remove it from the refrigerator. Pour the sesame seeds into a large sheet pan. Place the tuna loins into the pan and discard any remaining marinade. Roll the loins in the seeds to coat all sides.

Heat a seasoned skillet over medium-high heat for about 5 minutes or until it is hot. Pour the oil into the hot skillet and let it heat for 15 seconds.

Carefully place the tuna loins into the skillet in a single layer and cook them for 1½ minutes per side for rare (pink inside), turning them with tongs. Cook for 1 minute longer per side for medium. Remove the tuna from the skillet and transfer it to a clean platter. Cover it and refrigerate it for at least 1 hour. (If you are making multiple batches of this dish for a party, be sure to wipe the skillet clean after each batch, removing any blackened sesame seeds. Use fresh oil for the next batch.)

*Meanwhile, to prepare the wasabi sauce:* Whisk the mayonnaise, sour cream, mustard, lime juice, salt, and pepper in a medium glass or stainless steel bowl for 1 minute or until the mixture is smooth and well blended. Add the wasabi paste and whisk it in vigorously for 1 minute or until it is completely incorporated. Cover the sauce and refrigerate it for at least 30 minutes.

When you are ready to serve, scoop the sauce into a small bowl and set it in the center of a large serving platter. Remove the tuna from the refrigerator and place it on a work surface. Using a very sharp knife, slice the tuna into ¼-inch-thick medallions. Arrange the medallions on the platter around the sauce. Garnish the dish with fresh lime wedges.

*TIP: To season a new cast-iron skillet, you'll need ½ cup of peanut or canola oil. Preheat the oven to 350 degrees F. and wash and dry the skillet thoroughly. Grease the bottom and sides with 4 tablespoons of oil, wiping it with a paper towel to coat all the surfaces. Then place the skillet in the oven for 2 hours. With oven mitts, set the skillet on the stovetop to cool. Using another paper towel, wipe the inside clean with 2 more tablespoons of oil. Heat the skillet on a burner set to medium-high heat for 5 minutes. Turn off the heat, let the skillet cool, and then wipe it again with a fresh paper towel and 2 more tablespoons of oil. To clean a cast-iron pot, hand-wash it with just a little mild detergent. Rinse it and then wipe it with an oiled paper towel.*

*Time for Brunch: You can make the sauce up to 5 days in advance and refrigerate it, covered. Do not freeze it. Allow at least 2 hours for the tuna to marinate before cooking and 1 hour for it to chill afterward. You can cook the tuna up to 2 days in advance and refrigerate it, covered.*

# grilled and chilled jumbo shrimp with spicy tomato salsa

· · · · · · · · · · · · · · · · · · · · · · · · · · · · · · · · · · · · ·

*makes 36 shrimp*

*Marinating and then grilling gives these shrimp a double whammy of flavor, and instead of the usual cocktail sauce, our Spicy Tomato Salsa adds another flavor dimension. Be sure to make enough of these, because they go quickly.*

1 cup canola oil

Juice of 8 to 9 limes (about 1 cup)

¼ cup soy sauce

¼ cup honey

1 teaspoon kosher salt

¼ teaspoon freshly ground black pepper

36 jumbo (U-15) shrimp, thawed, peeled, and deveined, tail on

6 (12-inch) stainless steel or wooden skewers (if wooden, soaked in water for at least 30 minutes)

1 medium head Bibb or green-leaf lettuce, leaves separated, trimmed, washed, and dried

2 cups Spicy Tomato Salsa (see page 160), or tomato salsa from the supermarket's refrigerated section

4 limes, cut into wedges, for garnish

4 lemons, cut into wedges, for garnish

Fresh parsley sprigs, for garnish

> TIP: *Don't hesitate to buy frozen shrimp. Most of the shrimp available today, whether in the supermarket or the local seafood shop, is frozen and comes from one of the many shrimp farms around the world. To thaw frozen shrimp, just put it in a colander under running water. Do look for wild shrimp, which is usually frozen, too. It has better flavor and has not been fed antibiotics or hormones. Wild shrimp are becoming more widely available; ask your fishmonger to order them or buy them online. FYI, jumbo shrimp are sometimes called prawns.*

· · · · · · · · · · · · · · · · · · · · · · · · · · · · · · · · · · · · · · · · · · ·

Make a marinade by whisking the canola oil, lime juice, soy sauce, honey, salt, and pepper in a shallow glass or stainless steel baking dish. Place the shrimp into the dish in a single layer and turn them with tongs to coat all sides. Cover them and refrigerate them for at least 1 hour.

If you are using wooden skewers, immerse them completely in a container of water and soak them for at least 30 minutes.

Ten minutes before you plan to grill the shrimp, remove them from the refrigerator. Prepare a charcoal fire or preheat a gas grill to medium-high heat. Place the shrimp on a work surface and discard any remaining marinade. Thread 6 shrimp onto each skewer. Place the skewers on the grill in a single layer and grill them for 2 minutes per side. Transfer the skewers to a clean platter and let them cool for a few minutes.

Refrigerate the platter of shrimp, uncovered, for at least 30 minutes. (If you are cooking the shrimp more than 1 hour in advance, cover them with plastic wrap and refrigerate them until you are ready to serve.)

Line a serving platter with lettuce leaves. Pour the salsa into a small bowl and place it in the center of the platter. Pull the shrimp off the skewers and arrange them around the bowl. Garnish the shrimp with lemon and lime wedges and parsley sprigs.

*Time for Brunch: Allow at least 1 hour for the shrimp to marinate before grilling and 30 minutes for them to chill after grilling. You can grill the shrimp up to 1 day in advance, but they are best eaten the day you grill them.*

# grilled and roasted filet mignon with horseradish sauce

*makes 10 to 12 servings*

*I've served this dish at parties many, many times, and my guests always love it. The filet mignon is first grilled and then finished in the oven to maximize its flavor without overcooking it. The result is incredibly tender beef with a fragrance of garlic, herbs, and the grill that will drive your friendly carnivores wild. If you wish, you can make individual hors d'oeuvres by placing dabs of horseradish sauce and small slices of meat on bite-sized garlic toasts.*

### FILET MIGNON

¼ cup olive oil

4 medium cloves garlic, coarsely chopped

1 tablespoon finely chopped fresh parsley

1 tablespoon fresh rosemary leaves

1 tablespoon fresh thyme leaves

1 teaspoon kosher salt

¼ teaspoon freshly ground black pepper

4 pounds prime center-cut filet mignon

### HORSERADISH SAUCE

1½ cups mayonnaise, preferably Hellmann's

¾ cup sour cream

¼ teaspoon Worcestershire sauce

6 tablespoons bottled white horse-radish

¼ teaspoon kosher salt

⅛ teaspoon freshly ground black pepper

1 head red cabbage, hollowed-out, for serving sauce, optional

Grape tomatoes, for garnish

Whole garlic cloves, for garnish, peel on

Fresh sprigs parsley, rosemary and thyme, for garnish

*To prepare the filet mignon:* Make a marinade by whisking the olive oil, garlic, parsley, rosemary, thyme, salt, and pepper, in a small glass or stainless steel bowl. Place the filet mignon into a roasting pan. Pour the herbed oil over the filet, turn the meat with tongs to coat all sides, and rub it a little so that the oil penetrates it. Cover it and refrigerate it for at least 1 hour or overnight.

*To prepare the horseradish sauce:* Combine the mayonnaise, sour cream, Worcestershire sauce, horseradish, salt, and pepper in a small bowl and whisk the mixture vigorously for 1 minute or until it is smooth and well blended. Cover the sauce and refrigerate it until you are ready to serve.

Ten minutes before you plan to cook the filet, remove it from the refrigerator. Prepare a charcoal fire or preheat a gas grill to high. Preheat the oven to 375 degrees F. Place the filet on the grill, reserving the roasting pan and any remaining marinade. Sear the filet for 1 minute, then turn it with tongs and sear the other side for 1 minute. Repeat the process twice, cooking the filet for a total of 6 minutes or until it is nicely seared and marked. Transfer the filet back to the roasting pan.

Place the filet into the oven and roast it for 15 to 20 minutes or until an instant-read thermometer inserted into the center reads 130 degrees F. (for rare in the center). Remove the pan from the oven. Cover the meat with a piece of aluminum foil and let it rest for 5 minutes before carving it. (If you wish, cover it and refrigerate it for a few hours; then let it come to room temperature before serving.)

Spoon the sauce into a serving bowl or a hollowed-out red cabbage and place it in the center of a large serving platter.

Place the filet on a carving board and, using a sharp carving knife, carve the filet into medallions that are a little less than ½-inch thick. Arrange the medallions around the horseradish sauce. Garnish the platter with grape tomatoes, garlic cloves, and fresh herb sprigs.

*Time for Brunch: Allow at least 1 hour for marinating the filet, although you can marinate it overnight. This dish is delicious when the filet is grilled just before serving, but if you are pressed for time, you can grill it 1 day in advance, refrigerate it whole, covered, and then bring it to room temperature before you carve it. Any leftovers make great sandwiches, or just warm the meat in the oven for a few minutes and enjoy.*

# bowtie pasta with grilled portobello mushrooms and tomato-basil cream sauce

*makes 10 to 12 servings*

*Bowtie pasta is a nice complement to the big grilled portobello mushrooms in this dish, but you can substitute the pasta of your choice. If you don't want to fire up the grill, you can broil the mushrooms instead.*

4 large portobello mushroom tops

½ cup olive oil

1 tablespoon kosher salt, plus more to taste

Freshly ground black pepper to taste

1 pound bowtie pasta

4 cups Tomato-Basil Sauce (see page 162), or good-quality bottled tomato-basil sauce

2 cups half and half

1 cup pitted kalamata olives

6 large fresh basil leaves, cut in chiffonade

½ cup fresh chopped parsley

1 tablespoon dried oregano

1 cup freshly grated Parmesan cheese (4 ounces)

Fresh basil leaves, for garnish

---

*TIP: "Chiffonade" is the French term for cutting herbs and other vegetables into fine strips or "ribbons." To chiffonade basil, wash the leaves and pat them dry with paper towels. Then stack them one on top of the other and roll them lengthwise into a cylinder. Hold the roll with one hand and use a sharp chef's knife to slice it crosswise into ⅛-inch pieces. Or cut it with a pair of kitchen shears. Voilà! Unroll the pieces to find chiffonade.*

---

Prepare a charcoal fire, preheat the gas grill to high, or preheat the broiler.

Toss the mushrooms with the olive oil and season them with salt and pepper to taste. Grill or broil them for 4 minutes per side, turning them with tongs. Transfer the mushrooms to a work surface and let them sit for a few minutes until they are cool enough to handle. Slice them thinly.

Fill a large saucepan halfway with water. Add 1 tablespoon of salt and bring the water to a rolling boil over high heat. Add the bowtie pasta and cook it for 8 to 10 minutes or until it is al dente. Drain the pasta and set it aside for 1 minute.

In a large saucepan, heat the Tomato-Basil Sauce over medium heat, stirring it frequently, for 5 minutes. Whisk in the half and half. Add the olives, mushroom slices, basil, parsley, and oregano. Add the cooked pasta and toss it gently until all the ingredients are blended. Add all but 1 teaspoon or so of the Parmesan cheese and toss the pasta for 1 minute or until the cheese is melted.

To serve, spoon the pasta into a large warmed serving platter or chafing dish and garnish it with the remaining Parmesan cheese and basil leaves. Or transfer the pasta to an ovenproof casserole dish, cover it, and keep it warm in a 200-degree oven for up to 20 minutes. Garnish it with Parmesan and basil before serving.

*Time for Brunch: Make the basic Tomato-Basil Sauce, without the half and half, up to 3 days in advance. Grill the mushrooms up to 1 day in advance. Don't try to cook the pasta or assemble the dish until just before serving. You can hold the finished dish in a 200-degree oven for 15 to 20 minutes, but don't leave it much longer than that, or the pasta will get mushy.*

# penne with roasted fresh plum tomatoes and three cheeses

. . . . . . . . . . . . . . . . . . . . . . . . . . .

*makes 10 to 12 servings*

*Impress your friends with a fresh homemade tomato sauce that you make from scratch. They'll think you spent hours at the stove, but with our sauce, you roast the tomatoes and let your oven do the work. Grilled zucchini gives it a satisfying texture, while kalamata olives give it a little zip. If you're pressed for time and can't fire up the grill, you can broil the zucchini, but you'll lose that unmistakable grilled flavor.*

3 tablespoons plus a pinch of
    kosher salt

20 ripe medium-large plum
    tomatoes (about 4 pounds)

¾ cup extra-virgin olive oil

4 medium cloves garlic, coarsely
    chopped

1 cup pitted kalamata olives

2 teaspoons freshly ground black
    pepper, or to taste

3 medium zucchini, sliced
    lengthwise into ¼-inch slices

1 pound dried penne pasta

1 tablespoon dried oregano

10 large fresh basil leaves, sliced in
    chiffonade (see page 117)

½ cup grated Parmesan cheese
    (2 ounces)

½ cup grated Romano cheese
    (2 ounces)

½ cup grated Asiago cheese
    (2 ounces)

16 large fresh basil leaves, for
    garnish

Preheat the oven to 400 degrees F. Prepare a charcoal fire or preheat a gas grill to high.

    Fill a large saucepan halfway with water. Add 1 tablespoon of salt and bring the water to a rolling boil over high heat. Add the plum tomatoes and cook them for 1 to 2 minutes or until the skins begin to crack. Drain them in a large colander and rinse them with cold water. When the tomatoes are cool

. . . . . . . . . . . . . . . . . . . . . . . . . . . . . . .

enough to handle, peel the skin off with your hands. Place the peeled tomatoes into a smaller strainer and place a pot underneath to catch any juices. Let the tomatoes stand for 1 minute and then transfer them to a work surface. Trim and discard the tops and then cut the tomatoes in half. Squeeze out and discard any seeds and then cut the tomatoes in half again.

Put the tomato pulp into a large roasting pan and add ½ cup of olive oil, the garlic, the olives, 1 tablespoon of salt, and a little black pepper. Toss the mixture to blend all the ingredients and roast it in the oven, stirring it occasionally, for 15 minutes; then rotate the pan 180 degrees to ensure even roasting. Roast the mixture, stirring it occasionally, for 15 minutes longer.

Meanwhile, put the zucchini slices into a bowl and toss them with 1 tablespoon of olive oil and a pinch of salt and pepper. Place the zucchini slices on the grill in a single layer and grill them for 3 minutes per side. Transfer them to a clean platter and set them aside until they are cool enough to handle. Cut the slices into bite-sized pieces.

Fill a large saucepan halfway with water. Add 1 tablespoon of salt and bring the water to a rolling boil. Add the penne and cook it for 8 to 10 minutes or until it is al dente. Drain it in a colander, return it to the saucepan, and add 3 tablespoons of olive oil. Toss the pasta to coat it with the oil. Pour the roasted tomatoes over the pasta and set the pan over medium heat. Add the grilled zucchini, oregano, and basil chiffonade and season the mixture with pepper to taste. With a wooden spoon, fold it gently to blend all the ingredients. Add the Parmesan, Romano, and Asiago cheeses and stir the mixture gently for 1 minute or until they are melted.

If you are serving immediately, transfer the pasta to a large warmed serving bowl or chafing dish and garnish it with basil leaves. Or transfer it to a large ovenproof casserole, cover it, and keep it warm in a 200-degree oven for up to 45 minutes. Garnish it with basil leaves before serving.

*Time for Brunch: Make the roasted tomato sauce and grill the zucchini up to 2 days in advance. Don't try to cook the pasta or assemble the dish until just before serving. You can hold the finished dish in a 200-degree oven for 15 to 20 minutes, but don't leave it much longer than that, or the pasta will get mushy.*

# garden vegetable lasagna

*makes 10 to 12 servings*

*Years ago, when my customers asked for more vegetarian lunch entrees, I set out to make a lasagna that would include a bounty of veggies and cheeses. It's an utterly luscious and healthy meal—and a crowd-pleasing do-ahead dish for any party or family dinner.*

3 tablespoons olive oil

2 medium zucchini, sliced into
⅛-inch rounds and each round
cut into 2 half moons

2 medium yellow squash, sliced into
⅛-inch rounds and each round
cut into 2 half moons

1 (10-ounce) package baby bella
mushrooms. trimmed

2 pounds ricotta cheese

1½ cups grated Romano cheese
(6 ounces)

5 cups shredded mozzarella cheese
(1 pound)

2 large eggs

½ cup chopped fresh parsley

½ cup chopped fresh basil

2 teaspoons dried oregano

2 teaspoons kosher salt

2 teaspoons freshly ground black
pepper

8 cups Tomato-Basil Sauce (see
page 162), or good-quality
bottled tomato-basil sauce

1 (8-ounce) package no-boil lasagna
sheets

10 ounces frozen spinach, thawed
and drained well

Preheat the oven to 375 degrees F.

Heat the olive oil in a stockpot set over medium heat and swirl the pot to coat the surface. Add the zucchini, yellow squash, and mushrooms and sauté them, stirring them and shaking the pan frequently, for about 7 minutes or until they are softened. Remove the pot from the heat and drain the vegetables thoroughly.

In a large bowl, combine the ricotta and Romano cheeses, 3¾ cups of mozzarella cheese, and the eggs, parsley, basil, oregano, salt, and pepper. Mix the ingredients well to blend them.

To assemble the lasagna, pour 1½ cups of Tomato-Basil Sauce into a 9 × 13-inch ovenproof baking dish. Arrange a layer of lasagna noodles over the sauce, placing the pieces side by side. Top the noodles with half of the cheese mixture, another 1½ cups of sauce, and then half of the vegetable mixture. Top this with another layer of lasagna noodles and another 1½ cups of sauce. Top this with the remaining cheese mixture, the remaining vegetable mixture, and the spinach. Completely cover the top with lasagna noodles. Top them with 1 cup of sauce and the remaining 1¼ cups of mozzarella cheese. Cover the baking dish with aluminum foil, being careful not to allow the foil to rest on the top of the lasagna.

Bake the lasagna for 35 to 40 minutes or until an instant-read thermometer inserted into the center reads 165 degrees F. Remove the foil and bake the lasagna for 10 minutes longer or until the cheese is browned and melted. Remove the lasagna from the oven and let it rest for 10 to 15 minutes.

To serve, heat the remaining tomato sauce in a small saucepan on the stovetop over medium heat. Meanwhile, cut the lasagna into squares. Spoon some of the warm sauce on each plate and top it with a lasagna square. Spoon additional sauce over the lasagna if desired.

*Time for Brunch: Make the Tomato-Basil Sauce and/or the lasagna up to 3 days in advance and refrigerate it, covered. Reheat the lasagna in a 350-degree oven for 45 minutes to 1 hour or until an instant-read thermometer inserted into the center reads 165 degrees F.*

# 6 · bakery treats

## The Night Shift

Our bakers, like bakers everywhere, live an upside-down life. They work through the night when everybody else is sleeping—or, in the case of many Hamptons folk, playing—and get home to bed just in time for the rest of the world to start another day.

◄ Pear-Shaped Butter Cookies

The Golden Pear bakers pull their final batch of scones out of the oven around midnight and then load up our vans and set out to deliver their night's work to our cafes and wholesale clients, just at the hour when the glamorous Hamptons nightlife is at its peak. As they navigate the snarled nighttime traffic of our main artery, Montauk Highway, they get to watch the summer people partying the wee hours away. The revelers often gather en masse on the sidewalks in front of the most popular nightspots, so it's quite a show for whoever happens to be driving by.

By that time, the bakers — four skilled artisans — have put in a full night's work. They usually arrive at the bakeshop behind our Southampton cafe at four o'clock in the afternoon — no earlier or they'll get in the way of the day crew as they finish their shift (which begins at 6:00 A.M.). When the cooks leave, the bakers take over, working at full speed to produce the mind-boggling quantities of muffins, croissants, scones, cookies, and cakes that will be sold the following day. Once our six commercial ovens are fired up, they stay that way for the next eight or even ten hours.

The bakers' work follows strict Golden Pear standards: Use time-honored baking techniques — no shortcuts — and the freshest and best ingredients you can find, from butter and flour to fruit and chocolate. They're the same standards you'll want to follow in your kitchen, albeit with smaller quantities.

By 1:00 A.M. the baked goods have reached their destinations, and the bakers' work is done. They can head home, catch a few hours of sleep, and then — the nice thing about their upside-down hours — head for the beach. There, they can watch the parade of bathing beauties or, more likely, sleep a bit more, dreaming of the hundreds of muffins they baked the night before and the night before that.

# pear-shaped
# butter cookies

*makes 18 to 24 cookies*

*When it came time for us to create a signature cookie, of course it had to be in the shape of a pear. You can make these rich butter cookies in any shape you like; vary the shapes and colors with the seasons and the holidays. Naturally, we're partial to pears, and we make them all year round.*

2 sticks (1 cup) unsalted butter

1 cup granulated sugar

1 large egg

2 large egg yolks

2 teaspoons pure vanilla extract

3 cups all-purpose flour

2 teaspoons kosher salt

¼ cup colored sugar, available at gourmet stores and in the supermarket's baking department

> *TIP: When baking, make sure the butter and eggs are at room temperature, approximately 70 degrees F. This will allow the butter and sugar to cream (that is, blend until the mixture is light and fluffy), and allow the eggs to fully absorb into the creamed butter and sugar.*

Combine the butter and sugar in a mixing bowl. Using an electric mixer set at medium-low speed, mix them for 8 to 10 minutes or until the mixture is light and fluffy. (If you have a KitchenAid stand mixer, use the flat paddle attachment.) With a fork, gently beat the eggs, egg yolks, and vanilla in a small bowl until they are combined. Add the egg mixture to the butter mixture and mix them for 1 minute at medium speed. Stop the mixer to scrape down the side of the bowl and the beaters with a rubber spatula. Mix the ingredients for another 10 seconds.

In a separate bowl, combine the flour and salt and stir them just to blend them. Add the flour mixture to the butter mixture and mix them at low speed for 30 seconds.

Place a piece of plastic wrap on a work surface. Using a spatula, scoop the dough onto the plastic and fold it over to seal it. Flatten the wrapped dough into a 1½-inch-thick disk. Refrigerate it for at least 1 hour.

When you are ready to bake, position a rack in the center of the oven and preheat the oven to 375 degrees F. Line a 9 × 13-inch baking sheet with parchment paper. Flour a work surface.

If the dough has been in the refrigerator for 1 hour, unwrap it, place it on the work surface, and, with a floured rolling pin, roll it out to a thickness of ¼ inch. If the dough has been in the refrigerator longer than 1 hour, unwrap it and let it come to room temperature for about 30 minutes before attempting to roll it.

Using a pear-shaped cookie cutter (or any cookie cutter), cut out the cookies and place them on the baking sheet. Reroll the scraps and cut out more cookies to make a total of 18 to 24 cookies. Sprinkle them with colored sugar.

Bake the cookies for 8 minutes; then rotate the baking sheet 180 degrees to ensure even baking. Bake them for 8 minutes longer or until they are golden brown on the edges and slightly soft in the center. If you like crispier cookies, leave them in the oven for 1 to 2 more minutes.

Remove the baking sheet from the oven and, using a spatula, transfer the cookies to a wire rack to cool.

*Time for Brunch: You can store the cookie dough, wrapped in plastic, in the refrigerator for up to 5 days or freeze it for up to 1 month. Store the cookies in an airtight container for up to 5 days.*

# chocolate chip cookies

*makes 24 cookies*

*When I was a kid, the week before Christmas my mother would always bake hundreds of chocolate chip cookies. There would be large bowls of these delicious goodies all over our house, and my brothers and sister and I would feast on them into the new year. I've modified my mom's recipe just a touch, and we've been selling these from the day we opened.*

2 sticks (1 cup) unsalted butter, softened
¾ cup light brown sugar
¾ cup granulated sugar
2 large eggs
1 teaspoon pure vanilla extract

2¼ cups all-purpose flour
1 teaspoon baking soda
1 teaspoon kosher salt
1½ cups firmly packed highest-quality semisweet chocolate chips

> *TIP: Do you like your chocolate chip cookies chewy? Crispy? Two minutes more or less in the oven makes the difference. Either way, these cookies are delicious.*

Position a rack in the center of the oven. Preheat the oven to 375 degrees F. Place 2 nonstick 9 × 13-inch baking sheets on your work surface, or cover 2 regular 9 × 13-inch baking sheets with parchment paper.

Combine the butter and brown and granulated sugars in a mixing bowl. With an electric mixer set at low speed, mix them for 1 minute or until the mixture is light and fluffy. (If you have a KitchenAid stand mixer, use the flat paddle attachment.) Stop the mixer occasionally and scrape down the side of the bowl and the beaters with a rubber spatula.

Using a fork, gently beat the eggs and vanilla in a small bowl until they are just combined. Pour the egg mixture into the butter mixture and mix them at low speed until they are combined.

In a separate bowl, combine the flour, baking soda, and salt and stir them just to blend them. Add the flour mixture to the butter mixture all at once and mix them at low speed until they are combined. Add the chocolate chips and mix them in at low speed until they are combined.

With a teaspoon, spoon the batter onto the baking sheets, leaving about 2 inches between cookies. Bake the cookies for 5 minutes; then rotate the baking sheets 180 degrees to ensure even baking. Bake them for 5 minutes longer. (For crispier cookies, bake them for a total of 12 minutes.) Remove the cookies from the oven and cool them on the baking sheets for 5 minutes. Then, with a spatula, transfer the cookies to a wire rack to cool completely.

*Time for Brunch: Make these cookies up to 4 days in advance and store them in an airtight container. Freeze any leftovers, tightly wrapped in plastic, for up to 2 months.*

# chocolumps™

. . . . . . . . . . . . . . . . . . . . . . . . . .

*makes 54 small or 28 medium-large cookies*

*My wife, Anne, developed this delectable recipe years ago. I came up with the name one day as I was baking them. Hmm, I said to myself, chocolaty, lumpy . . . Chocolumps™! They're equally good whether you serve them as a snack, on your brunch dessert tray, or with your after-dinner coffee.*

½ stick (¼ cup) unsalted butter

4 ounces unsweetened chocolate

4 cups firmly packed highest-quality semisweet chocolate chips

4 large eggs

1½ cups granulated sugar

1½ teaspoons pure vanilla extract

⅓ cup plus 2 tablespoons all-purpose flour

½ teaspoon baking powder

¼ teaspoon kosher salt

4½ teaspoons instant espresso

3 cups chopped walnuts

⅔ cup shelled whole walnuts, each lobe cut in half

Position a rack in the center of the oven. Preheat the oven to 300 degrees F. Place 2 nonstick 9 × 13-inch baking sheets on your work surface, or line 2 regular nonstick 9 × 13-inch baking sheets with parchment paper.

In a double boiler set over medium heat, melt the butter, the unsweetened chocolate, and 2 cups of chocolate chips. Remove the pot from the heat and let the mixture cool for 2 minutes.

Combine the eggs and sugar in a mixing bowl. Using an electric mixer set at medium speed, mix them for about 5 minutes or until the mixture is a very pale yellow. (If you have a KitchenAid stand mixer, use the flat paddle attachment.) Add the vanilla and the melted chocolate mixture and mix them in at low speed until they are blended. Stop the mixer occasionally and scrape down the side of the bowl and the beaters with a rubber spatula.

In a separate bowl, combine the flour, baking powder, salt, and espresso powder and stir them just to blend them. Add the flour mixture to the chocolate mixture and mix them at low speed for about 30 seconds. Stop the mixer and scrape down the side of the bowl and the beaters. Add the remaining 2 cups

. . . . . . . . . . . . . . . . . . . . . . . . . . . . . . . . . . .

of chocolate chips and the chopped walnuts and mix them in at low speed for about 30 seconds. Using the spatula, mix the batter by hand to make sure all the ingredients are thoroughly blended.

Working in batches, use a tablespoon or ½-ounce scoop to spoon the batter onto the baking sheets, spacing the cookies about 2 inches apart. Place a walnut piece in the center of each cookie. Bake the cookies for 10 minutes; then rotate the baking sheets 180 degrees to ensure even baking. Bake them for 10 minutes longer. Remove the cookies from the oven and cool them on the baking sheets for 10 minutes. Then, with a spatula, transfer the cookies to a wire rack to cool completely. Repeat the process with the remaining batter. Cool the cookies on the rack for 1 to 1½ hours. The cookies should still be soft and chewy when they are cool.

*Time for Brunch: Make Chocolumps™ up to 4 days in advance and store them in an airtight container. Freeze any leftovers, tightly wrapped in plastic, for up to 2 months.*

# oatmeal raisin cookies

*make 36 cookies*

*A Golden Pear Cafe favorite, our heart-healthy oatmeal cookies go the extra mile: They're made with oat bran and rolled oats, and the honey makes them wonderfully moist and chewy. Not to worry—though they're a healthy snack, they're delicious, too.*

2 sticks (1 cup) unsalted butter, softened

1 cup packed brown sugar

¼ cup granulated sugar

¼ cup honey

2 large eggs

1¼ teaspoons pure vanilla extract

1 cup all-purpose flour

1 cup oat bran

2⅔ cups rolled oats (not instant oatmeal)

¾ teaspoon baking soda

¾ teaspoon ground cinnamon

1¼ cups raisins

Position a rack in the center of the oven. Preheat the oven to 375 degrees F. Place 2 nonstick (9 × 13-inch) baking sheets on your work surface or line 2 (9 × 13-inch) baking sheets with parchment paper.

Combine the butter, brown and granulated sugars, and honey in a mixing bowl. Using an electric mixer set at low speed, mix them for 8 to 10 minutes or until the mixture is light and creamy. (If you have a KitchenAid stand mixer, use the flat paddle attachment.) Stop the mixer occasionally and scrape down the side of the bowl and the beaters with a rubber spatula.

Using a fork, gently beat the eggs and vanilla in a small bowl until they are combined. Pour the egg mixture into the butter mixture and mix them at medium speed until they are combined. Do not overmix. Scrape down the side of the bowl and the beaters as necessary.

In a separate bowl, combine the flour, oat bran, rolled oats, baking soda, and cinnamon and stir them just to blend them. Add the flour mixture to the butter mixture and mix them at low speed for about 1 minute. Add the raisins and mix the batter until it forms a dough.

Spoon the dough by heaping tablespoons onto the baking sheets, spacing the cookies about 2 inches apart to make 18 cookies per sheet. Press down on each cookie lightly, leaving space for the cookies to spread.

Bake the cookies for 7 minutes; then rotate the baking sheets 180 degrees to ensure even baking. Bake them for 7 minutes longer. Remove the cookies from the oven and cool them on the baking sheets for 5 minutes. Then, with a spatula, transfer the cookies to a wire rack to cool completely.

*Time for Brunch: Make these cookies up to 4 days in advance and store them in an airtight container. Freeze any leftovers, tightly wrapped in plastic, for up to 2 months.*

# amazing chocolate
# walnut brownies

*makes 16 brownies*

*One late Saturday afternoon, a couple sat down on the bench in front of the Golden Pear in Southampton. It was a beautiful, sunny day, and they sat for a while, talking quietly and holding hands. The bench faces away from the cafe, out to the street, so we couldn't see their faces, but it was obvious that they were absorbed in each other. After a while, the woman came into the Golden Pear, poured two coffees, and ordered some brownies to go. Arms full of treats, she returned to her friend. It was only then that I noticed that the guy was the Boss—Bruce Springsteen—enjoying a low-key, anonymous afternoon. I liked the idea that he and his friend chose our brownies for a relaxing snack. If you're a brownie lover—or just in love—this is the ultimate recipe: fudgy, chewy, and chocolaty, with just the right proportion of nuts. Share these with someone you care about.*

Nonstick vegetable oil spray
1 cup all-purpose flour
½ teaspoon baking soda
½ teaspoon kosher salt
¼ cup canola oil
1 stick (½ cup) unsalted butter
¼ cup water, preferably filtered

3½ cups firmly packed highest-
  quality semisweet chocolate
  chips
1⅓ cups granulated sugar
4 large eggs
1½ teaspoons pure vanilla extract
1 cup chopped walnuts

*TIP: The secret to our delicious brownies is that we use very high-quality chocolate chips. Shop around and do some tasting to find a brand you really like.*

Position a rack in the center of the oven. Preheat the oven to 350 degrees F. Spray a 9 × 13-inch baking pan with nonstick vegetable oil spray.

Combine the flour, baking soda, and salt in a mixing bowl and stir them just to blend them. Set the mixture aside.

In a double boiler set over medium heat, heat the canola oil, butter, water, chocolate chips, and sugar, whisking the mixture occasionally, until the chocolate and butter are melted, all the ingredients are blended, and the mixture is smooth.

Pour the hot chocolate combination into a mixing bowl. Using a fork, gently beat the eggs and vanilla in a small bowl until they are combined. Using an electric mixer set at low speed, slowly add the egg mixture to the chocolate mixture and mix them until they are blended. (If you have a KitchenAid stand mixer, use the flat paddle attachment.) Do not overmix. Slowly add the flour mixture and mix it in at low speed until all the ingredients are combined. Stop the mixer occasionally and scrape down the side of the bowl and the beaters with a rubber spatula.

Using a rubber spatula, fold in the walnuts until they are completely incorporated into the batter.

Scrape the batter into the pan and smooth the surface with a rubber spatula. Bake it for 20 minutes; then rotate the pans 180 degrees to ensure even baking. Bake it for 20 minutes longer. Remove it from the oven and let it cool in the pan on a wire rack before cutting it into 16 squares and "diving in."

*Time for Brunch: Make these brownies up to 4 days in advance and store them in an airtight container. Freeze any leftovers, tightly wrapped in plastic, for up to 2 months.*

# blondies

· · · · · · · · · · · · · ·

*makes 16 blondies*

A not-too-distant cousin to our famous brownies, these blondies are rich and redolent of caramel. Those who want an alternative to brownies will love these buttery beauties. We serve them side by side with brownies for dessert at catering functions and, let me tell you, they fly off the platter.

Nonstick vegetable oil spray

1½ sticks (¾ cup) unsalted butter, softened

1¾ cup packed brown sugar

1 tablespoon plus ¾ teaspoon canola oil

2 large eggs

2 teaspoons pure vanilla extract

2 cups all-purpose flour

1¾ cup baking powder

¾ teaspoon kosher salt

1 cup firmly packed highest-quality semisweet chocolate chips

1½ cups chopped walnuts

> *TIP: Few ovens heat evenly, so when you're baking it's important to rotate your pan 180 degrees halfway through the baking time. Otherwise, half a batch might come out overdone and the other half underdone.*

Position a rack in the center of the oven. Preheat the oven to 350 degrees F. Spray a 9 × 13-inch baking pan with nonstick vegetable oil spray.

Combine the butter, brown sugar, and oil in a large mixing bowl. With an electric mixer set at medium speed, mix them for 5 to 6 minutes or until the mixture is smooth and light tan in color. (If you have a KitchenAid stand mixer, use the flat paddle attachment.) Using a fork, gently beat the eggs and vanilla in a small bowl until they are combined. Add the egg mixture to the butter mixture and mix them at medium speed until they are combined. Stop the mixer occasionally and scrape down the side of the bowl and the beaters.

In a separate bowl, combine the flour, baking powder, and salt and stir them just to blend them. Add the flour mixture to the butter mixture and mix them at low speed for about 30 seconds. Scrape down the side of the bowl as

· · · · · · · · · · · · · · · · · · · · · · · · · · · · · · · · · · · · · · · · · · · · · · · · · · · ·

necessary. Increase the speed to medium and mix the batter for about 30 seconds.

Using a wooden spoon or rubber spatula, fold in the chocolate chips and 1 cup of chopped walnuts and stir the batter until they are completely incorporated.

Scrape the batter into the pan and smooth the surface with a rubber spatula. Sprinkle the remaining ½ cup of walnuts on top of the batter. Bake it for 20 minutes; then rotate the pan 180 degrees to ensure even baking. Bake it for 15 minutes longer or until it is golden on the top and soft inside. Remove it from the oven and let it cool in the pan on a wire rack. Cut it into 16 squares.

*Time for Brunch: Make these blondies up to 4 days in advance and store them in an airtight container. Freeze any leftovers, tightly wrapped in plastic, for up to 2 months.*

# chocolate pecan bars

*makes 16 bars*

When Rob Tebinka joined our team as executive chef in the spring of 2003, I asked him to create another bar-type dessert that would stand up next to our brownies and blondies. He nailed it with this one! His Chocolate Pecan Bars give you all the pleasure of an ooey-gooey chocolaty pecan pie, but because you can eat them with your fingers, they're ideal for buffets and picnics at the beach.

Nonstick vegetable oil spray

PECAN–CHOCOLATE CHIP
TOPPING
½ cup chopped pecans
1 cup firmly packed highest-quality
    semisweet chocolate chips

CRUST
2¼ cups all-purpose flour
⅓ cup granulated sugar
¾ teaspoon kosher salt
1¼ sticks (½ cup plus 2
    tablespoons) cold unsalted
    butter, cut into small pieces
3 tablespoons whole milk

PECAN FILLING
1¾ sticks (¾ cup plus
    2 tablespoons) unsalted butter
1 cup brown sugar
⅓ cup honey
3 tablespoons whole milk
1 tablespoon pure vanilla extract
½ teaspoon kosher salt
3 cups chopped pecans

Position a rack in the center of the oven. Preheat the oven to 350 degrees F. Spray a 9 × 13-inch pan with nonstick vegetable oil spray.

*To begin preparing the topping:* Spread ½ cup of pecans on a baking sheet. Bake them for 10 minutes or until they are golden and fragrant. Remove them from the oven and set them aside.

*Meanwhile, to prepare the crust:* Combine the flour, sugar, and salt in a mixing bowl. Using an electric mixer set at low speed, mix them for 30 seconds. (If you have a KitchenAid stand mixer, use the flat paddle attachment.)

Add the butter and mix it in at low speed for 5 to 6 minutes or until it is almost completely incorporated and the mixture takes on the consistency of cornmeal. Add the milk and mix it in at low speed for 2 to 4 minutes or until large crumbs form. Press the crumbs into the bottom of the pan, making the edge slightly higher but not extending up the entire side of the pan. Bake the crust for 20 to 25 minutes or until it is very lightly browned.

*To prepare the filling:* Melt the butter with the brown sugar, honey, milk, vanilla, and salt in a saucepan set over medium heat. Cook the mixture, stirring it frequently, for about 3 minutes or until it reaches a simmer. Add the pecans and cook it for about 1 minute or until it begins to simmer again. Remove the pan from the heat and set it aside.

When the crust is baked, pour the warm filling into it. Bake it for 15 to 20 minutes longer or until the filling bubbles in the center and the crust is slightly darker around the edges. Transfer the pan to a wire rack.

Sprinkle the chocolate chips on top and allow them to melt. Using a rubber spatula, spread the melted chocolate over the entire surface. Sprinkle the toasted pecans evenly over the top. Cool it for about 2 hours or to room temperature. Cut it into 16 bars.

*Time for Brunch: Make these bars up to 5 days in advance and store them in an airtight container or tightly wrapped in plastic.*

# blueberry crumb cake

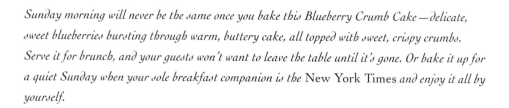

*makes 2 (8½ × 4-inch) loaves*

*Sunday morning will never be the same once you bake this Blueberry Crumb Cake—delicate, sweet blueberries bursting through warm, buttery cake, all topped with sweet, crispy crumbs. Serve it for brunch, and your guests won't want to leave the table until it's gone. Or bake it up for a quiet Sunday when your sole breakfast companion is the New York Times and enjoy it all by yourself.*

Nonstick vegetable oil spray

### CRUMB TOPPING
2 cups all-purpose flour
¾ cup brown sugar
¾ cup granulated sugar
3 teaspoons ground cinnamon
½ teaspoon kosher salt
2 sticks (1 cup) cold unsalted
   butter, cut into ½-inch cubes

### BLUEBERRY CAKE
1¾ sticks (¾ cup plus 2
   tablespoons) unsalted butter
1½ cups granulated sugar
2 large eggs
3½ cups all-purpose flour, sifted
   after measuring, plus 2 teaspoons
   for coating blueberries
2½ teaspoons baking powder
½ teaspoon kosher salt
1¼ cups whole milk
2 teaspoons pure vanilla extract
¾ pint fresh blueberries (1½ cups),
   washed in a fine-mesh strainer
   and drained

Position a rack in the center of the oven. Preheat the oven to 350 degrees F. Spray 2 (8½ × 4-inch) loaf pans with nonstick vegetable oil spray.

***To prepare the crumb topping:*** Pour the flour, brown sugar, granulated sugar, cinnamon, and salt into a bowl. Using an electric mixer set at low speed, mix the ingredients until they are combined. (If you have a KitchenAid stand mixer, use the flat paddle attachment.) Add the butter and mix it in at medium-low speed for about 5 minutes or until the mixture takes on the consistency of coarse crumbs. Transfer the crumb topping to a small bowl and set it aside.

*To prepare the cake:* Wipe off the mixer blades. Combine the butter and sugar in a mixing bowl. With the mixer set at medium speed, mix them for 8 to 10 minutes or until the mixture is light and fluffy. Using a fork, gently beat the eggs in a small bowl. Add them to the butter mixture and mix this at medium speed for 1 minute. Stop the mixer occasionally and scrape down the side of the bowl and the beaters with a rubber spatula.

Measure out 3½ cups of flour and sift it into a large bowl. Add the baking powder and salt and stir the ingredients just to blend them. Add one-third of the flour mixture to the butter mixture and mix them at low speed until the flour is completely incorporated. Add ½ cup plus 2 tablespoons of milk and 1 teaspoon of vanilla and mix them in at low speed until they are completely incorporated. Increase the speed to medium and mix the batter for 30 seconds. Scrape down the side of the bowl after each addition as necessary. Add one-third of the flour mixture and mix it in at low speed until it is completely incorporated. Add the remaining milk and 1 teaspoon of vanilla and mix them in at low speed until they are incorporated. Increase the speed to medium and mix the batter for 30 seconds. Add the remaining flour mixture and mix it in at low speed until it is completely incorporated. Increase the speed to medium and mix the batter for 1 minute.

Place the blueberries into a bowl and sprinkle them with the remaining 2 teaspoons of flour. Toss them gently to coat them. Using a rubber spatula, fold the blueberries into the batter.

Scrape the batter into the loaf pans, dividing it evenly between them and smoothing the surfaces with a rubber spatula. Sprinkle half of the crumb topping on each loaf.

Bake the cakes for 35 minutes; then rotate the pans 180 degrees to ensure even baking. Bake them for 30 minutes longer or until a toothpick inserted into the center of each cake comes out clean. Cool the cakes in the pans for 20 minutes before removing them from the pans.

*Time for Brunch: Make these cakes up to 4 days in advance and store them in an airtight container. Freeze any leftovers, tightly wrapped in plastic, for up to 2 months.*

# chocolate–chocolate chip loaf cake

*makes 2 (8½ × 4-inch) loaves*

*Here's a cake for true chocolate lovers: moist, dense, chocolate cake, filled with yummy chocolate chips. It's a perfect calorie splurge for brunch. Don't hesitate to slice this cake and top it with fresh raspberries or sliced strawberries.*

Nonstick vegetable oil spray

5¾ ounces unsweetened chocolate

2 cups all-purpose flour, sifted after measuring, plus more for dusting

2 sticks (1 cup) unsalted butter, softened

2 cups granulated sugar

4 large eggs

½ teaspoon baking powder

½ teaspoon baking soda

½ teaspoon kosher salt

¾ cup sour cream

2 teaspoons pure vanilla extract

1¼ cups firmly packed highest-quality semisweet chocolate chips

Position a rack in the center of the oven. Preheat the oven to 350 degrees F. Spray 2 (8½ × 4-inch) loaf pans with nonstick vegetable oil spray and flour them lightly, tapping out any excess.

In a double boiler set over medium heat, melt the chocolate. Remove the pot from the heat and set it aside to cool.

Combine the butter and sugar in a large mixing bowl. With an electric mixer set at medium speed, mix them for 8 to 10 minutes or until the mixture is light and fluffy. (If you have a KitchenAid stand mixer, use the flat paddle attachment.) Using a fork, gently beat the eggs in a small bowl. Add them to the butter mixture and mix them in at medium speed for 1 minute. Stop the mixer occasionally and scrape down the side of the bowl and the beaters with a rubber spatula. Add the cooled chocolate and mix it in at low speed until it is thoroughly incorporated.

Measure out 2 cups of flour and sift it into a mixing bowl. Add the baking powder, baking soda, and salt and stir the ingredients just to blend them. Add half of the flour mixture to the butter mixture and mix it in low speed until it is completely incorporated. Increase the speed to medium and mix the batter for 30 seconds. Scrape down the side of the bowl after each addition as necessary. Add the sour cream and vanilla and mix them in at low speed until they are completely incorporated. Increase the speed to medium and mix the batter for 15 seconds. Add the remaining flour mixture and mix it in at low speed until it is incorporated. Increase the speed to medium and mix the batter for 30 seconds.

Using a rubber spatula, fold in the chocolate chips until they are completely incorporated.

Scrape the batter into the loaf pans, dividing it evenly between them and smoothing the surfaces with a rubber spatula. Bake the cakes for 30 minutes; then rotate the pans 180 degrees to ensure even baking. Bake them for 35 minutes longer or until a toothpick inserted into the center of each cake comes out clean. Cool the cakes in the pans for 20 minutes before removing them from the pans.

*Time for Brunch: Make these cakes up to 4 days in advance and store them in an airtight container. Freeze any leftovers, tightly wrapped in plastic, for up to 2 months.*

# lemon loaf cake

*makes 2 (8½ × 4½-inch) loaves*

*Back in 1988, my wife, Anne, created this luscious lemony confection, with its irresistible topping of lemon glaze and coarse sugar. We can't keep enough of them on the shelf. The recipe calls for cake flour, which gives the loaf a lighter, more crumbly texture. Cake flour is made from soft wheat and is chlorinated to break down the gluten. It's usually much whiter than all-purpose flour, and it feels soft and smooth between your fingers.*

Nonstick vegetable oil spray

**LEMON CAKE**

1¾ sticks (¾ cup plus
   2 tablespoons) unsalted butter

2 cups granulated sugar

2 large eggs

Grated zest of 1 lemon (about
   2 tablespoons)

3 cups cake flour, sifted after
   measuring

1½ teaspoons baking powder

1½ teaspoons kosher salt

Juice of 1 lemon (about
   2 tablespoons)

1 cup plus 3 tablespoons whole milk

**LEMON GLAZE**

Juice of 3 to 4 lemons (about
   ½ cup), strained several times to
   remove all pulp

½ cup granulated sugar

3 tablespoons coarse or large-grain
   granulated sugar, for topping

> *TIP: When a recipe calls for both lemon zest and juice, you don't need separate lemons for each. Zest the lemon first, using a zester, which you can find at any cooking supply store, and then squeeze the juice out. Note that for this recipe, you'll need four to five lemons—one for the juice and zest in the cake and the rest for the juice in the glaze. Note also that we specify that the juice for the glaze must be strained. You should, of course, strain all fresh lemon juice to remove the seeds, but for this glaze, we strain it a few times so that it is perfectly clear and free of pulp.*

Position a rack in the center of the oven. Preheat the oven to 350 degrees F. Spray 2 (8½ × 4½-inch) loaf pans with nonstick vegetable oil spray.

*To make the cake:* Combine the butter and sugar in a large mixing bowl. Using an electric mixer set at medium speed, mix them for 8 to 10 minutes or until the mixture is light and fluffy. (If you have a KitchenAid stand mixer, use the flat paddle attachment.) Using a fork, gently beat the eggs in a small bowl. Add the eggs to the butter mixture and mix them at medium speed for 1 minute. Add the lemon zest.

Measure out the cake flour and sift it into a separate mixing bowl. Add the baking powder and salt and stir the ingredients just to blend them. Add one-third of the flour mixture to the butter mixture and mix them at low speed for about 1 minute or until the flour is completely incorporated. Add the lemon juice and 1 cup plus 1½ tablespoons of milk. Mix them in at low speed until they are completely incorporated. Stop the mixer and scrape the side of the bowl and the beaters with a rubber spatula after each addition. Increase the mixer speed to medium and mix the batter for 30 seconds. Add one-third of the flour mixture and mix it in at low speed for 1 minute. Add the remaining milk and mix it in until it is incorporated. Increase the mixer speed to medium and mix the batter for 30 seconds. Add the remaining one-third of the flour mixture and mix it in at low speed for 1 minute or until it is completely incorporated. Increase the speed to medium and mix the batter for 1 minute.

Scrape the batter into the loaf pans, dividing it evenly and smoothing the surfaces with a spatula. Bake the cakes for 35 minutes; then rotate the pans 180 degrees to ensure even baking. Bake them for 30 minutes longer or until a toothpick inserted into the center of each cake comes out clean.

*While the cakes are baking, make the glaze:* Cook the lemon juice and sugar in a small saucepan set over high heat until the mixture comes to a boil. Immediately remove it from the heat and keep it warm.

When the cakes are done, remove them from the oven and use a pastry brush to spread each with half of the glaze. Sprinkle 1½ tablespoons of coarse sugar on each cake. Cool the cakes in the pans for 20 minutes before removal.

*Time for Brunch: Make these cakes up to 4 days in advance and store them in an airtight container. Freeze any leftovers, tightly wrapped in plastic, for up to 2 months.*

# pumpkin loaf cake
. . . . . . . . . . . . . . . . . . . . . . . . . . . . . .

*makes 2 (8½ × 4½-inch) loaves*

*I love to see the farmlands in and around the Hamptons dotted with bright orange globes. Pumpkins are my consolation prize when every other sign tells me that another beautiful summer has come to an end. This extra-moist loaf fits my definition of having your cake and eating it, too: You might find yourself baking it up just because it makes your whole house smell so good! When it comes out of the oven, though, you'll definitely want to eat it.*

Nonstick vegetable oil spray

3 cups all-purpose flour, sifted after measuring, plus more for dusting and coating

2 sticks (1 cup) unsalted butter

1 cup granulated sugar

⅔ cup packed light brown sugar

2 large eggs

1 cup canned pumpkin (not pumpkin pie filling)

4 teaspoons baking powder

2 teaspoons baking soda

½ teaspoon kosher salt

½ teaspoon ground ginger

½ teaspoon ground cinnamon

⅛ teaspoon grated nutmeg

2 teaspoons pure vanilla extract

½ cup plus 2 tablespoons whole milk

⅔ cup raisins

Position a rack in the center of the oven. Preheat the oven to 350 degrees F. Spray 2 (8½ × 4½-inch) loaf pans with nonstick vegetable oil spray and flour them lightly, tapping out any excess.

Combine the butter and granulated and brown sugars in a large mixing bowl. Using an electric mixer set at medium speed, mix them for 8 to 10 minutes or until the mixture is blond in color and fluffy. (If you have a KitchenAid stand mixer, use the flat paddle attachment.) Using a fork, gently beat the eggs in a small bowl. Add them to the butter mixture and mix them in at medium speed for 1 minute. Add the pumpkin and mix it in at medium speed until it is thoroughly incorporated.

In a separate bowl, combine 3 cups of flour with the baking powder, baking soda, salt, ginger, cinnamon, and nutmeg and stir the ingredients just to blend them. Add half of the flour mixture to the butter mixture and mix it in

. . . . . . . . . . . . . . . . . . . . . . . . . . . . . . . . . . . . . . . . . . . . . . . . . . . .

at low speed until it is thoroughly incorporated. Add the milk and mix it in at low speed to combine it. Increase the speed to medium and mix the filling for 15 seconds longer. Stop the mixer and scrape the side of the bowl and the beaters with a rubber spatula after each addition. Add the remaining flour mixture and mix it in at low speed until it is well blended. Increase the speed to medium and mix the filling for 30 seconds.

Place the raisins into a cup, add ½ teaspoon of flour, and mix them to coat the raisins lightly, tapping off any excess. With a rubber spatula, fold the raisins into the batter.

Scrape the batter into the loaf pans, dividing it evenly between them and smoothing the surfaces with a rubber spatula. Bake the cakes for 25 minutes; then rotate the pans 180 degrees to ensure even baking. Bake them for 25 minutes longer or until a toothpick inserted into the center of each cake comes out clean. Cool the cakes in the pans for 20 minutes before removing them from the pans.

*Time for Brunch: Make these cakes up to 4 days in advance and store them in an airtight container or wrapped in plastic. Freeze any leftovers, tightly wrapped in plastic, for up to 2 months.*

# sour cream loaf cake

. . . . . . . . . . . . . . . . . . . . . . . . . . . . . . . . . . . . . . . . .

*makes 2 (8½ × 4½-inch) loaves*

*An old-fashioned sour cream cake, rich, yet tender, and utterly luscious. If you think it doesn't get any better than this, add the optional cup of chocolate chips; they complement the buttery cake perfectly.*

**Nonstick vegetable oil spray**

**SOUR CREAM CAKE**
**1¾ sticks (¾ cup plus 2 tablespoons) unsalted butter**
**2 cups granulated sugar**
**2 large eggs**
**3 cups cake flour, sifted after measuring**
**1½ teaspoons baking powder**

**1½ teaspoons kosher salt**
**1 cup sour cream**
**2 teaspoons pure vanilla extract**
**1 cup firmly packed highest-quality semisweet chocolate chips, optional**

**CINNAMON-SUGAR TOPPING**
**½ teaspoon ground cinnamon**
**1 tablespoon granulated sugar**

Position a rack in the center of the oven. Preheat the oven to 350 degrees F. Spray 2 (8½ × 4½-inch) loaf pans with nonstick vegetable oil spray.

***To make the cake:*** Combine the butter and sugar in a large mixing bowl. Using an electric mixer set at medium speed, mix them for 8 to 10 minutes or until the mixture is light and fluffy. (If you have a KitchenAid stand mixer, use the flat paddle attachment.) Using a fork, gently beat the eggs in a small bowl. Add them to the butter mixture and mix them in at medium speed for 1 minute. Stop the mixer occasionally and scrape the side of the bowl and the beaters with a rubber spatula.

In a separate bowl, combine the cake flour, baking powder, and salt and stir them just to blend them. Add half of the flour mixture to the butter mixture and mix it in at low speed for 1 minute or until it is completely incorporated. Increase the speed to medium and mix the batter for 30 seconds. Scrape down the side of the bowl after each addition as necessary. Add the

. . . . . . . . . . . . . . . . . . . . . . . . . . . . . . . . . . . . . . . . .

sour cream and vanilla and mix them in at low speed for 30 seconds or until they are incorporated. Increase the mixer speed to medium and mix the batter for 30 seconds. Add the remaining flour mixture and mix it in at low speed for about 30 seconds or until it is completely incorporated. Increase the speed to medium and mix the batter for 1 minute.

Add the chocolate chips, if you're using them, and fold them into the mixture with a rubber spatula to distribute them evenly.

Scrape the batter into the loaf pans, dividing it evenly between them and smoothing the surfaces with a rubber spatula.

*To prepare the topping:* In a small bowl, mix the cinnamon and sugar until they are well blended. Sprinkle half of the topping on each of the filled loaf pans.

Bake the cakes for 25 minutes; then rotate the pans 180 degrees to ensure even baking. Bake them for 30 minutes longer or until a toothpick inserted into the center of each cake comes out clean. Cool the cakes in the pans for 20 minutes before removing them from the pans.

*Time for Brunch: Make these cakes up to 4 days in advance and store them in an airtight container or tightly wrapped in plastic. Freeze any leftovers for up to 2 months, tightly wrapped in plastic.*

# apple crumb pie

*makes 1 (9½-inch) deep-dish pie*

*After our annual postsummer slowdown, along comes Thanksgiving week, and suddenly it feels like summer again in the bakery, if only for a few days. Our executive chef, Rob, gears up for the onslaught of orders for these holiday pies, and by the time Thanksgiving Day arrives, he and his crew have assembled and baked a few hundred. Fortunately, we're closed Thanksgiving Day, so they can rest up after all that furious baking. Be sure to allow six hours of cooling time before you cut into it.*

## CRUST

1½ sticks (¾ cup) cold unsalted
    butter, cut into small pieces
2 cups all-purpose flour
⅓ cup ice water, preferably filtered

## CRUMB TOPPING
*(MAKES ABOUT 4 CUPS)*

1⅔ sticks cold unsalted butter, cut
    into small pieces
1¾ cups all-purpose flour
⅓ cup granulated sugar
¾ cup packed light brown sugar
⅓ cup rolled oats (not instant
    oatmeal)
⅓ cup shelled walnuts, coarsely
    chopped
¼ teaspoon ground cinnamon

## APPLE FILLING

8 to 10 Cortland or Granny Smith
    apples, peeled, cored, and cut
    into ¼-inch slices (about 8 cups)
¼ cup granulated sugar
¼ cup brown sugar
¼ stick (2 tablespoons) unsalted
    butter, melted
½ teaspoon lemon zest
½ teaspoon fresh lemon juice
1 tablespoon cornstarch
¼ teaspoon ground cinnamon
Pinch of grated nutmeg
⅛ teaspoon kosher salt

***To prepare the crust:*** Combine the butter and flour in a mixing bowl. Using an electric mixer set at low speed, mix them for 3 to 5 minutes or until most of the butter is incorporated into the flour. (If you have a KitchenAid stand mixer, use the flat paddle attachment.) Add the ice water and mix it in at low speed for about 1 minute or until a dough begins to form. Transfer the dough to a work surface and, using your hands, form it into a ball. Cover it with plastic wrap and let it rest in a cool spot for 30 minutes.

*Meanwhile, to prepare the crumb topping:* Combine the butter, flour, granulated and brown sugars, rolled oats, walnuts, and cinnamon. Roll the mixture with your hands until small crumbs form and the butter is completely incorporated into the other ingredients. Set the topping aside.

Place the dough on a work surface and roll it into a 12-inch circle. Then roll the circle around your rolling pin, pick it up, and unroll it, centered, over a 9½-inch deep-dish pie plate. With your fingers, tuck the dough into the pan and up the side and flute the edge. Trim the edge to make it even. Set the crust aside.

*To prepare the filling:* Combine the apples, granulated and brown sugars, melted butter, lemon zest and juice, cornstarch, cinnamon, nutmeg, and salt in a large mixing bowl and, using a rubber spatula, mix them until they are blended.

Preheat the oven to 350 degrees F. Pour the filling into the crust and spread the apples evenly with a spatula. Sprinkle the crumb topping over the surface, covering all the apples.

Bake the pie for 40 minutes; then rotate the pan 180 degrees to ensure even baking. Bake it for 40 minutes longer or until an instant-read thermometer inserted into the center of the pie reads 185 to 190 degrees F. Watch carefully; if the crumb topping browns before the baking time has elapsed, cover it with aluminum foil for the remainder of the baking time. Cool the pie thoroughly (at least 6 hours) before cutting it.

*Time for Brunch: Make this pie up to 4 days in advance and store it in an airtight container. Allow 6 hours of cooling time before you cut it. Freeze any leftovers, tightly wrapped in plastic, for up to 2 months.*

# pumpkin pie

*makes 1 (9½-inch) deep-dish pie*
*(8 to 10 servings)*

*Bake this pie and your entire house will fill with the tantalizing aroma of pumpkin and spices. The recipe calls for a "blind-baked" piecrust—that is, a piecrust that is first baked empty and then filled. To blind-bake, you'll need a pound of dry beans or some baking weights; these will keep the bottom of the crust from bubbling and becoming uneven.*

### CRUST

1½ sticks (¾ cup) cold unsalted
    butter, cut into small pieces
2 cups all-purpose flour
⅓ cup ice water, preferably filtered

### PUMPKIN FILLING

3 large eggs
¼ cup granulated sugar
½ cup light brown sugar

1 (15-ounce) can pumpkin (not
    pumpkin pie filling) (about
    2 cups)
1 teaspoon ground cinnamon
⅛ teaspoon grated nutmeg
¾ teaspoon ground ginger
⅛ teaspoon ground cloves
½ teaspoon kosher salt
2 cups heavy cream

***To prepare the crust:*** Combine the butter and flour in a mixing bowl. Using an electric mixer set at low speed, mix them for 3 to 5 minutes or until most of the butter is incorporated into the flour. (If you have a KitchenAid stand mixer, use the flat paddle attachment.) Add the ice water and mix it in at low speed for about 1 minute or until a dough begins to form. Transfer the dough to a work surface and, using your hands, form it into a ball. Cover it with plastic wrap and let it rest in a cool spot for 30 minutes.

***Meanwhile, to prepare the filling:*** Using a wire whisk, beat the eggs in a large mixing bowl. Whisk the granulated and brown sugars into the eggs. Whisk in the pumpkin, cinnamon, nutmeg, ginger, cloves, and salt. Gradually whisk in the cream and continue whisking until all of the ingredients are incorporated. Set the filling aside.

Place the dough on a work surface and roll it into a 12-inch circle. Then roll the circle around your rolling pin, pick it up, and unroll it, centered, over a 9½-inch deep-dish pie plate. With your fingers, tuck the dough into the pan and up the side and flute the edge. Trim the edge to make it even. Prick the bottom of the crust with a fork 10 to 12 times. Place the crust into the freezer and chill it for 15 to 20 minutes.

Position a rack in the center of the oven. Preheat the oven to 375 degrees F. Remove the crust from the freezer and line the inside with aluminum foil or parchment paper. Fill it with dry beans or baking weights. Bake the crust for 15 minutes. Remove the crust from the oven and carefully remove the beans or weights and the foil or parchment. Bake the crust for 10 minutes longer or until it is very lightly browned.

Remove the crust from the oven and pour the filling into it. (Or, if you are freezing the crust for use on another day, let it cool and then wrap it in plastic and freeze it for up to 2 months.) Return the pie to the center rack of the oven and bake it for about 1 hour or until a toothpick inserted into the center of the pie comes out clean. Cool the pie completely before slicing it.

*Time for Brunch: You can prepare the crust 1 to 2 days in advance, cover it loosely with foil, and store it in a cool, dry place until you're ready to fill it. Or wrap it well in plastic wrap and freeze it for up to 2 months. Remove it from the freezer 2 hours before you plan to bake it. Once you assemble and bake the pie, it will keep in the refrigerator for up to 3 days. Just don't try to freeze it once it's filled.*

# 7 · golden pear basics

In the past few years, the Hamptons have become a culinary center in their own right. Innovative chefs and fabulous restaurants flourish in these beach communities because there is an eager, sophisticated client base to support them (although, just as in major cities, restaurants

◄ Golden Pear Guacamole with Organic Tortilla Chips

come and go, and the cast changes every few seasons). Quality and freshness reign supreme here, and there's also a demand for virtuoso technique and whatever the cutting-edge ingredient of the moment might be.

The Golden Pear has been part of this food scene since our opening in 1987. In fact, we're probably one of the longer-lived establishments with a claim to higher culinary aspirations. While I spend much of my time now managing the business and leading my excellent team, I still love the food part of it, and I get into the kitchen whenever I can to create new recipes.

Most of the recipes in this book are the result of sitting and thinking about food. Over the years, I developed a habit of thinking about which ingredients we could combine to create something delicious. Whether it was a salad, a chili, a soup, a muffin, or a main dish, I'd think about the basics and build on them with colorful, tasty twists. I hope the basics here will encourage you to do the same and to create your own recipes with which to delight and tantalize your family and friends.

# golden pear
# chicken stock

*makes 2¾ quarts*

*Use this savory stock as a base for soups or sauces. Trade secret: Don't stir the stock while cooking, or it will become cloudy. Start with a five-pound roasting chicken or a rotisserie chicken from the supermarket. Remove the meat from the bones and use it for chicken soup, salad, or sandwiches. Save the carcass for the stock.*

Carcass of 1 (5-pound) chicken

5 quarts cold water, preferably filtered

1 medium onion, cut into 1-inch pieces

2 medium carrots, cut into 1-inch pieces

4 large stalks celery, including leaves, cut into 1-inch pieces

½ bay leaf

5 to 6 black peppercorns

½ bunch fresh parsley

> *TIP: If you are roasting the chicken from scratch, season it with salt, pepper, and fresh rosemary leaves and roast it in a preheated 375-degreee oven for 1½ hours or until an instant-read thermometer inserted into the thickest part of the thigh reads 165 degrees F. When the chicken is cool enough to handle, remove the meat from the bones and eat it right away or refrigerate it for another use.*

Place the chicken carcass into a 10-quart stockpot with a cover. Add the water and set it over high heat. Cover it and bring it to a boil. Uncover the pot and reduce the heat to a simmer. Simmer it, occasionally skimming any scum from the surface with a slotted spoon, for 15 minutes.

Add the vegetables to the pot and simmer it, uncovered, occasionally skimming any scum from the surface, for 1 hour. Add the bay leaf, peppercorns, and parsley and simmer it for 1 hour longer. Remove it from the heat.

Place a colander over a large mixing bowl and strain the stock into it. Reserve the liquid and discard the solids. Strain the stock again through a fine-mesh strainer, reserving the liquid. Skim any fat from the surface.

Cover the stock and refrigerate it or freeze it in small portions. You can use an ice cube tray for freezing, then pack the cubes into airtight containers or resealable plastic freezer bags.

*Time for Brunch: This stock will keep in the refrigerator for 3 days or in the freezer for 3 months.*

# golden pear vegetable stock

*makes 8 to 9 cups*

*When you're making vegetarian dishes, this is the stock to use. It's great in soup, sauces, and chili. In fact, you can use it any time chicken stock is called for. The turnip and parsnip give it a nice body and complexity.*

3 quarts cold water, preferably filtered

1 large white onion, cut into 1-inch pieces (about 2 cups)

3 medium carrots, cut into 1-inch pieces (about 2 cups)

4 large stalks celery, leaves included, cut into 1-inch pieces (about 2 cups)

2 small turnips, peeled and cut into 1-inch pieces (about 1 cup)

2 medium parsnips, peeled and cut into 1-inch pieces (about 2 cups)

6 to 7 whole black peppercorns

1 medium bunch fresh parsley, including stems (about 2 cups)

2 teaspoons kosher salt

Pour the water into a 6-quart stockpot and add the onion, carrots, celery, turnips, and parsnips, peppercorns, and parsley. Set the pot over high heat and bring it to a boil. Boil it for about 12 minutes; then reduce the heat to a simmer and simmer it for 30 minutes. Do not overcook the stock, or it will become bitter.

Place a colander over a large mixing bowl and strain the stock into it. Reserve the liquid and discard the solids. Stir in the salt and let the stock cool.

Cover the stock and refrigerate it or freeze it in small portions. You can use an ice cube tray for freezing, then pack the cubes into airtight containers or resealable plastic freezer bags.

*Time for Brunch: This stock will keep in the refrigerator for 3 days or in the freezer for 3 months.*

# balsamic vinaigrette

. . . . . . . . . . . . . . . . . . . . . . . . . . . . . . . . .

*makes ½ cup*

*Balsamic vinegar is mild, with a nice, light sweetness that makes a lovely vinaigrette. It's just right for savory salads like our Balsamic Chicken Salad. Use it on just about any salad that needs an easy, perky dressing. If you need more, just increase the ingredients proportionately.*

**6 tablespoons extra-virgin olive oil**
**2 tablespoons balsamic vinegar**
**1 teaspoon fresh chopped basil**

**¼ teaspoon kosher salt**
**Pinch of freshly ground black**
**pepper**

Whisk the olive oil, balsamic vinegar, basil, salt, and pepper in a glass or stainless steel bowl until they are thoroughly combined.

*Time for Brunch: Make the dressing up to 3 days in advance and store it, covered, in the refrigerator. Stir it well before using it.*

# citrus vinaigrette

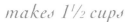

*makes 1½ cups*

*This tangy dressing is just bursting with flavor. We use it in our Citrus Veggie Tuna Salad and to liven up any combination of mixed greens. It's wonderful on a warm summer day; the citrus makes a lip-smacking complement to whatever you pair it with.*

¾ cup canola oil

Juice of 2 to 3 lemons (about 5 tablespoons), or more to taste

Juice of 1 lime (1½ to 2 tablespoons)

2 tablespoons fresh chopped parsley

1 tablespoon fresh chopped thyme leaves

1 teaspoon fresh chopped oregano

2 teaspoons coarse-grain mustard

1 teaspoon kosher salt, or more to taste

Freshly ground black pepper to taste

In a glass or stainless steel bowl, whisk the canola oil, lemon and lime juices, parsley, thyme, oregano, mustard, salt, and pepper until they are thoroughly blended. Taste the dressing and season it with more salt and pepper if needed.

*Time for Brunch: Make the dressing up to 3 days in advance and store it, covered, in the refrigerator. Stir it well before using it.*

# spicy tomato salsa

*makes 3 cups (8 to 10 servings)*

*We use this zesty salsa in our Southwestern Grilled Chicken Wrap and as a dip with tortilla chips. You can use it for any number of Southwestern- or Mexican-style dishes; it's so much better than the jarred stuff you find at the supermarket. You can turn the heat up or down to suit your personal taste by adjusting the quantity of hot pepper sauce that you add.*

10 ripe medium plum tomatoes, seeded and finely chopped (about 5 cups)

2 medium yellow bell peppers, seeded and finely chopped (about 1½ cups)

2 medium green bell peppers, seeded and finely chopped (about 1½ cups)

½ small red onion, finely chopped (about ½ cup)

2 cloves garlic, finely chopped (about 2 tablespoons)

1 (6-ounce) can tomato paste (¾ cup)

2 tablespoons balsamic vinegar

Juice of 1 lime (1½ to 2 tablespoons)

¼ teaspoon hot pepper sauce such as Tabasco, or to taste

½ cup chopped fresh cilantro

1 teaspoon kosher salt

¼ teaspoon freshly ground black pepper

Combine the tomatoes, yellow and green bell peppers, onions, and garlic in a large glass or stainless steel bowl.

Combine the tomato paste, balsamic vinegar, lime juice, hot pepper sauce, cilantro, salt, and pepper in a food processor fitted with a metal blade. Process the ingredients until they are blended. Add this mixture to the tomato mixture and mix them thoroughly. Cover the salsa and refrigerate it for at least 1 to 2 hours. Let it stand at room temperature for 15 to 25 minutes before serving.

***Time for Brunch:** Make this salsa up to 1 day in advance. Store any leftovers in the refrigerator, covered, for up to 4 days.*

# guacamole

*We use this chunky guacamole on sandwiches, in wraps, and as a dip with tortilla chips. It can be used as an accompaniment to all kinds of dishes—but you might just want to eat it with a spoon, all by itself! Remember that avocados turn brown when exposed to air, so it's important to coat them with an acidic ingredient—in this case lime juice—as soon as you cut them.*

8 ripe Haas avocados
Juice of 4 limes (about ½ cup)
1 medium clove garlic, minced
¼ cup canned diced roasted green chili peppers, drained well
⅛ teaspoon hot pepper sauce such as Tabasco

2 teaspoons kosher salt
½ teaspoon freshly ground black pepper
½ cup finely chopped fresh cilantro leaves

Cut the avocados in half lengthwise. With a sharp knife, make a cut in the pit. Carefully twist the knife; the pit should come out easily. Spoon the pulp out of the skin and place it in a medium mixing bowl. Crush the pulp with your hands or the back of a wooden spoon. Add the lime juice and toss the avocado to coat it.

Add the garlic, chili peppers, hot pepper sauce, salt, pepper, and cilantro and toss the mixture to combine the ingredients. Cover the guacamole and refrigerate it for at least 1 to 2 hours. Remove it from the refrigerator 30 minutes before serving.

*Time for Brunch: Make this guacamole up to 1 day in advance. Add a little fresh lime juice just before serving to freshen it up.*

# tomato-basil sauce

*makes about 2 quarts*

*Every winter, my brother and I rent a ski house in Stratton, Vermont, for a few weekends to get away with our wives and children. I always make this sauce for the gang after a long day on the slopes, and a much needed soak in the hot tub. Serve this sauce with the Golden Pear's Garden Vegetable Lasagna or the Bowtie Pasta with Grilled Portobello Mushrooms and Tomato-Basil Cream Sauce—or any other pasta you like. It's also great with penne, cavatelli, homemade pizza, or meatball or sausage sandwiches.*

2 tablespoons olive oil

½ medium Spanish onion, chopped
   (about 1 cup)

5 medium cloves garlic, chopped
   (about 3 tablespoons)

1 (35-ounce) can Italian plum
   tomatoes

1 (8-ounce) can tomato paste
   (1 cup)

1 cup water, preferably filtered

2 tablespoons granulated sugar

½ cup chopped fresh basil

¼ cup chopped fresh parsley

1 tablespoon dried oregano

1 tablespoon kosher salt, or to taste

1 teaspoon freshly ground black
   pepper, or to taste

> *TIP: For a delicious meat sauce, add 1 cup of browned ground beef or ground turkey and 1 cup of cooked chopped sweet Italian sausage to the finished recipe and simmer it for another 15 minutes.*

Heat the olive oil in a medium saucepan set over medium heat and swirl the pan to coat the surface. Add the onions and sauté them, stirring them occasionally, for about 5 minutes, or until they are soft and translucent. Add the garlic and cook the mixture, stirring it and shaking the pan, for about 1 minute or until the garlic is softened.

Combine the tomatoes, tomato paste, and water in a blender or a food processor fitted with a metal blade and pulse it 5 times for 2 seconds at a time or until the mixture takes on the consistency of a coarse puree.

Pour the tomato mixture into the saucepan with the onion mixture, add the sugar, and stir the sauce to blend all the ingredients. Increase the heat and bring it to a boil. Immediately reduce the heat and simmer it for about 10 minutes. Stir in the basil, parsley, oregano, salt, and pepper and simmer it for 15 minutes. Taste the sauce and season it with more salt and pepper if necessary.

*Time for Brunch: Make this sauce up to 3 days in advance and refrigerate it, covered. Or freeze it in an airtight container for up to 2 months.*

# rosemary focaccia

*makes 1 (11 × 17-inch) focaccia*

*A sandwich is only as good as the bread it's served on. Here's a savory bread that will make all your sandwiches winners—and it's perfect to serve in your bread basket at the dinner table. Your guests will be impressed with your artisanal skill.*

1½ cups warm water, preferably filtered (no higher than 110 degrees F.)

1 teaspoon granulated sugar

2½ teaspoons (1 envelope) active dry yeast

3½ cups unbleached all-purpose flour, plus more for dusting

1½ cups whole-wheat flour

2 teaspoons table salt

7 tablespoons olive oil

3 tablespoons plus 1 teaspoon chopped fresh rosemary leaves

1 cup whole milk

1 teaspoon kosher salt

> *TIP: Yeast is a living thing. Once you mix your yeast with sugar and water and let it stand for five minutes, if it doesn't foam, discard it and try another package. It's dead.*

Pour the water into a small bowl, add the sugar and yeast, and whisk the ingredients together. Let the mixture stand for 5 minutes or until the yeast begins to foam.

Combine the yeast mixture, 3½ cups of flour, the whole-wheat flour, the table salt, 3 tablespoons of olive oil, the whole milk, and 3 tablespoons of rosemary in a large mixing bowl. Using an electric mixer set at low speed, mix the ingredients for 2 to 3 minutes or until they are blended and a dough forms. (If you have a KitchenAid stand mixer, use the flat paddle attachment.)

Grease a large bowl with 1½ teaspoons of olive oil. Flour a work surface lightly and turn out the dough onto it. Knead the dough: Press it away from you with the heels of your hands; then fold it in half and press it again. Repeat the process 6 to 7 times; then roll the dough to form a smooth ball. Place the dough into the prepared bowl, cover it tightly with plastic wrap, and let it rise in a warm spot for about 1 hour or until it is doubled in size.

Grease an 11 × 17-inch jelly roll pan (sheet pan) with 1½ teaspoons of olive oil. Turn the dough out onto it and pat and press the dough until it covers the entire surface of the pan in a fairly even layer. Dimple the surface with your fingertips. Drizzle it with the remaining 3 tablespoons of olive oil and use a pastry brush to spread the oil evenly. Sprinkle the dough with the kosher salt and 1 teaspoon of fresh rosemary. Set it aside and let it rise for about 1 hour (or more if needed) until it is doubled in size.

Preheat the oven to 450 degrees F. Position a rack in the lower third of the oven. Bake the focaccia for about 12 minutes; then lift a corner of it up with a spatula to make sure the bottom isn't becoming too brown. If it is too dark, place a second pan (of the same size) upside down under the pan. Bake the focaccia for 13 minutes longer and remove it from the oven. Remove it from the pan and cool it on a wire rack.

*Time for Brunch: This focaccia is best made the same day you plan to serve it. Freeze any leftovers, tightly wrapped in plastic, for up to 2 months.*

# sourdough bread

*makes 1 (8- or 9-inch round loaf)*

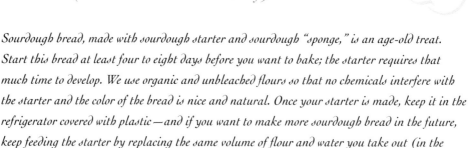

*Sourdough bread, made with sourdough starter and sourdough "sponge," is an age-old treat. Start this bread at least four to eight days before you want to bake; the starter requires that much time to develop. We use organic and unbleached flours so that no chemicals interfere with the starter and the color of the bread is nice and natural. Once your starter is made, keep it in the refrigerator covered with plastic—and if you want to make more sourdough bread in the future, keep feeding the starter by replacing the same volume of flour and water you take out (in the original proportions).*

SOURDOUGH STARTER
2 cups organic all-purpose flour
1 cup water, preferably filtered

SOURDOUGH SPONGE
1 cup warm water, preferably
    filtered (no higher than
    110 degrees F.)
1 cup sourdough starter
2 cups all-purpose unbleached flour

SOURDOUGH BREAD
2 tablespoons olive oil
1½ to 1¾ cups all-purpose
    unbleached flour
Sourdough sponge (entire recipe
    above)
2 teaspoons kosher salt

> *TIP: Place a roasting pan half full of water on the bottom of the oven when you bake this bread. This produces a steamy baking environment, which helps to create a crispy crust.*

*To prepare the sourdough starter:* Mix 1 cup of flour and ½ cup of water in a mixing bowl and set it, uncovered, in a warm, clean spot. After a couple of days the mixture should bubble and have a slightly sour smell. If it smells really foul and not just sour, it's no good; throw it away and start again in a clean bowl.

Once the mixture has bubbled, "feed" it with another 1 cup of flour and ½ cup of water. Stir it to incorporate the additions and transfer the mixture to a glass or plastic container. Cover it with plastic wrap and refrigerate it for 3 to 7 days.

*To prepare the sourdough sponge:* At least 8 hours before you plan to bake, mix 1 cup of warm water, 1 cup of sourdough starter, and 2 cups of all-purpose unbleached flour in a mixing bowl. Cover it with plastic and let it rise in a warm (not hot) spot for at least 8 hours or overnight. (Overnight is best.)

*To prepare the bread:* Flour a work surface and grease a large bowl with 1 tablespoon olive oil. Grease an 8- or 9-inch springform pan with the remaining olive oil and flour it lightly, tapping out any excess. Set it aside.

Combine the whole sourdough sponge with 1½ cups of flour and the salt in a large mixing bowl. Using an electric mixer set at low speed, mix them until a dough begins to form and stick to the beaters. (If you have a KitchenAid stand mixer, use the flat paddle attachment.) If the dough is too sticky, add some or all of the remaining ¼ cup of flour and mix it in to incorporate it. Turn out the dough onto the floured work surface and knead it, pressing it with the heel of your hand and folding it over, 6 or 7 times. Finish by forming it into a smooth ball.

Place the dough in the prepared bowl and turn it over a few times so that all sides are coated with oil. Cover the dough and let it rise in a warm spot for 2 to 4 hours or until it is doubled in size. Carefully transfer the dough to the prepared springform pan. Cover it with plastic wrap and allow it to rise again for 1 to 2 hours or until it is doubled in size.

Position a rack in the center of the oven and preheat the oven to 450 degrees F. Dust the top of the dough with a little flour. Using a sharp knife, make three diagonal ¼- to ½-inch-deep cuts along the top of the loaf. Make 3 more cuts in the opposite direction to form a lattice pattern.

Place a metal pan (not a baking sheet) in the bottom of the oven. Fill it with water halfway up the sides, being careful not to burn yourself with hot steam that may rise from it. Place the springform pan on the center rack and bake the bread for 20 minutes; then reduce the oven temperature to 375 degrees F. Bake the bread for 20 to 30 minutes longer or until it is browned on top. Remove it from the pan and cool it on a wire rack.

*Time for Brunch: This bread is best made the same day you plan to serve it. Freeze any leftovers, tightly wrapped in plastic, for up to 2 months.*

# appendix

After many years and countless catering jobs, I've learned a thing or two about entertaining. I've observed a little bit about human nature as it applies to entertaining, too. Simply put, planning a party is fun for some but overwhelming for others. My advice: Go for the fun. That doesn't mean you

◄ Grilled and Chilled Jumbo Shrimp with Spicy Tomato Salsa

don't have to prepare. What kind of party do you want to give? This book is about brunch, so we'll stick to that, but even within the parameters of a brunch format, there's a wide range of possibilities.

## What Kind of Party?

Will you go formal or casual? Buffet or sit-down? Will it be a big affair or an intimate gathering for just a friend or two? If it's big, do you have enough of your own equipment, dishware and glassware?

If you're reading this cookbook, you obviously want to get into the kitchen, but are you going to do all the food yourself? Or will you supplement home cooking with some store-bought or catered items? No guilt if the answer is yes; be honest with yourself about your time, your budget, and your stress level and consider my advice about fun.

In the same vein, can you hire service staff from a reputable service company, so that you're free to mingle with your guests and enjoy your party? What kinds of decorations or flowers do you have in mind? Is it a theme party, at which the food and décor will support a particular concept?

## What Food Will You Serve?

Once you know what kind of party you're giving, it's time to plan the menu. Think about your guests and the foods they might enjoy. It's a good idea to have some classic, familiar dishes—prepared with a flair, of course—as well as some that are a little more daring. Unless you have unlimited time to spend cooking, some dishes should be relatively simple do-aheads; then you can lavish attention on one or two labor-intensive, wow-eliciting items. Nor should you assume that the simple do-aheads must be dull! Lots of times, the simplest dishes are the dazzlers.

What I like about brunch is that you can serve a delicious variety of foods. A classic brunch menu includes a selection of fresh baked goods; a warm egg-based dish such as quiche or frittata; a platter of smoked fish; a selection of fresh salads such as fresh fruit, chicken, tuna, pasta and/or mixed greens; and an assortment of sandwiches. These days, though, anything goes, and your guests will likely be thrilled with everything from New England Beef Stew to Chilled Jumbo Shrimp with Spicy Tomato Salsa. Vegetarian options, like our Garden Vegetable Lasagna, are always a thoughtful touch.

## What Drinks Will You Offer?

Brunch, by its very nature (it's one part breakfast and one part lunch), calls for fine brewed coffee and juice. Special coffee drinks, such as our cafe mocha, lend a festive air. If you wish, offer alcoholic drinks. You can go with a seasonal punch and/or sparkling wines, alone or mixed with fruit and fruit juices. You can even go all out with a full bar.

For coffee, count on brewing at least one cup per person. Not everyone will drink tea, but you can show you care about those who do by having a carafe of hot water and a selection of fine teas at your coffee station. For alcoholic drinks, figure one per person per hour. If you're serving wine, each bottle contains about six glasses. If you're doing a full bar, don't forget mixers: club soda, tonic, ginger ale, and orange and tomato juices. Or garnishes; lemon, lime, and orange slices, and olives for martinis. And ice: about half a pound per person, more in hot weather. Whatever your bar style, do also serve plenty of bottled water, sparkling water, cola, diet cola, lemon-lime soda, and fruit juice for nondrinkers or folks who've had enough of the strong stuff.

## Stay Safe

Especially when you're planning a buffet, at which foods will sit out for a time, don't forget food safety.

Be sure to cook all hot foods to a temperature of 160 degrees F., the point at which salmonella and a host of other foodborne bacteria will be destroyed.

Don't place cooked food back on plates that have held raw foods, as any raw juices can contaminate the cooked food.

Don't use a marinade as a dipping sauce or condiment unless you heat it to boiling and boil it for a few minutes to kill any bacteria that leached into the marinade from the meat, poultry, or fish that was sitting in it.

Don't use knives, cutting boards, bowls, or any cooking implements that you've used on raw animal protein for other foods that will not be cooked. In other words, don't use the same knife to cut up salad that you've already used to cut and trim your raw chicken; don't use a cutting board on which you've pounded beef as a work surface to prepare crudités or canapés.

When it's time to serve, use warming trays or chafing dishes (best set at 140 degrees F.) to keep hot foods hot. Use ice to keep cold foods cold (place platters of food atop large rimmed platters of crushed ice) or wrap cold packs in decorative linens and place food platters on them.

Don't let hot or cold foods sit out on a buffet for more than three hours. If you're going to save leftovers, be sure to refrigerate them immediately.

## A Final Thought

I hope this book's recipes and helpful hints guide you in planning and executing your next brunch or other gathering. Of course, you could prepare many of these recipes for your personal enjoyment, too. Preparing good food and entertaining guests is a rewarding experience, whether you're a novice or an expert. My wife and I enjoy throwing a party and inviting friends and family to our home, even if it's not a special occasion and just for fun. Getting people together and serving them good food makes for happy times, and it builds fond memories to boot. I hope you enjoy the experience with these treats from the Golden Pear Cafe. Bon appétit!

# index